Kathleen invites you to move through serious abusive trauma, and come out the other end. Interestingly enough, I now know two women who from childhood experienced sexual trauma and both of these women have spent a lifetime consciously healing. The result in each of them is an amazing depth of wisdom, awesome articulation and way shower for so many others. Both have lived a life of generous service for others who have known this level of physical and psychological pain.

- *Marilyn Nyborg*

My Indomitable Heart will crack you open down the middle from page one. It is all at once a surge of hope, an uprising of faith and an olive branch extended into the depths of our soul for all those who have trespassed us. It is the great reminder of those who have traveled this path - that Love is greater than fear. I cannot recommend or sing the praises of this book any louder! - *Aletheia Pistis Sophia, author of Sacred Sexual Union*

Kathleen's book is an inspiration and a demonstration of the essence of resiliency. How her love provided the impetus for healing traumas that were unimaginable to endure, much less overcome. She emboldens us all to step into our own courage and offer our love to the world.
- *Patrcia Fero LMSW, Author of What Happens When Women Wake Up? What Happens When Women Converge? Sacred Marching Orders*

Kathleen's wise memoir points the way to a life of personal power and sovereignty to anyone brave enough to heed the call of their heart. While your story and path will be as individual as you are, this courageous journey of healing from physical and emotional abuse demonstrates the power of listening to and following your own heart's wisdom. -   *Gail Larsen, teacher and author of Transformational Speaking: If You Want to Change the World, Tell a Better Story*

In Kathleen's book, My Indomitable Heart, we are blessed with a remarkable authentic journey of deep sexual abuse and her many heartfelt healings. She repeatedly learned especially not to be controlled by those who abused her. A well written book filled with courageous inspirational heart healings. To all who have had similar abuse she has powerful practices for your heart healing heart. -   *Patt Lind-Kyle award winning author of Embracing the End of Life*

I was honored to assist Kathleen as she finessed her astonishing story. It is raw and powerful, deeply moving and revealing. The shocking experiences are balanced with moments of sheer wonder, synchronicity, and magic. Be prepared to take a journey like no other as a young girl experiences betrayal, murder, and abuse. Yet, through it all, she continues to love. This book will challenge your sensitivities, provide hope and inspiration, and open your heart to more love. It is a heroine's journey that can serve and support women on the healing path. -   *Kerani Marie, author and artist, Underworld Womb Journey, and Inner Wisdom Guide*

Kathleen's book is an inspiration and a demonstration of the essence of resiliency. How her love provided the impetus for healing traumas that were unimaginable to endure, much less overcome. She emboldens us all to step into our own courage and offer our love to the world. -   *Patricia Fero, LMSW, author of What Happens When Women Wake Up?, What Happens When Women Converge?, and Sacred Marching Orders*

MY INDOMITABLE HEART

Love Awakening To Love

KATHLEEN PLANT LOY

Copyright © 2024 Kathleen Plant Lov

ALL RIGHTS RESERVED. This book contains material protected under International and Federal Copyright Laws and Treaties. Any unauthorized reprint or use of this material is prohibited. No part of this book may be reproduced or transmitted in any form or by any means, electronic or mechanical, including photocopying, recording, or by any information storage and retrieval system, without express written permission from the author/publisher.

ISBN: 979-8-89079-302-7 (paperback)
ISBN: 979-8-89079-303-4 (ebook)

This book is dedicated to my beloved son, Ben

Ben has always had a quiet confidence and presence of being in the moment. He is extremely creative and talented, and an amazing artist. Ben is about being real, being true. He is a very loving, wonderful, dedicated partner and father. He has always been a teacher for me and I humbly bow to him with immense gratitude for being my son. I feel so much freedom and gratitude in my heart for the way he has broken the chains of abuse that had been passed on for so many generations.

TABLE OF CONTENTS

Chapter 1: One Billion Rising Speech 1

Chapter 2: Introduction 3

Chapter 3: Losing My Power 9

Chapter 4: Camino De Santiago 34

Chapter 5: Emotionally Devastated 40

Chapter 6: My Father – The Murder 42

Chapter 7: Growing up 47

Chapter 8: My Mother 59

Chapter 9: Nevada City 70

Chapter 10: Divorcing Richard 73

Chapter 11: My Freedom 79

Chapter 12: Returning to Nevada City 100

Chapter 13: India 105

Chapter 14: My True India Family 119

Chapter 15: Caring for my Mother 123

Chapter 16: Sedona Magic 127

Appendix: Powerful Practices 137

CHAPTER ONE

ONE BILLION RISING SPEECH

Several years ago, I was asked to give the "survivor" speech for One Billion Rising in my community of Nevada City/Grass Valley California. The statistics are that one of every three women will be beaten or sexually molested in her lifetime. With more than 8 billion people now on our planet, that adds up to well over a billion women! One Billion Rising takes place all over the world every year on Valentine's Day. I remember it was an unusually warm evening. A huge group of people walked along the streets and then we were all dancing to break the chains!

All the people were now seated and it was time for me to share my story. You could hear the wind whisper as I began. As I spoke at the One Billion Rising gathering that evening, even men had tears in their eyes. I had done decades of healing work around all of the abuse in my life. And yet it seems there are always more layers and layers.

I was surprised how calm I felt speaking of all of this for the first time to a group of people from my community. I feel it is important we release the stories that have been held underground, so they can be healed.

It is with that hope and desire that I now share my story with you through this book. I hope it gives you the courage for what you need in your life. And to keep your heart opened to love. Love is the great healer.

CHAPTER TWO

INTRODUCTION

Hold my hand as I share my story with you……

This book is for you, my dear sisters, girlfriends, friends, women of all ages, sizes, colors, shapes, beliefs, attitudes, all around the world. Also, to the men who have been abused and want to heal. We are one under the sun.

This is the story of my life; facing horrific events throughout my years growing up and how I didn't get defeated or subdued, which is what indomitable means. Choosing to move forward in my life with curiosity and fearlessness, I discovered Love awakening to Love. I never stopped loving. Throughout it all I was by the grace of the Divine Mother able to keep my heart open and filled with love.

KATHLEEN PLANT LOV

Love is patient;
Love is kind;
Love is not envious or boastful or
Arrogant or rude.
It does not insist on its own way;
it is not irritable or resentful;
it does not rejoice in wrongdoing,
but rejoices in the truth.
It bears all things, believes all things,
hopes all things, endures all things.
Corinthians 13,4-7

It has been a dark time on Mother Earth for a very long time, but now we are entering not only the Aquarian Age but a whole new 26,000-year cycle. How exciting is that! Hold my hand, dear one, as we begin our journey. The time of having our voices silenced, truth squelched, being dominated by others' power is coming to an end. There is a blurring of this top-down, power-over-others old paradigm, and the new emerging paradigm is that we all have a voice, and we work together in community to build and create this new earth.

Magical creatures like mermaids, mermen, fairies, and leprechauns who have hidden to stay safe now come out to join our hearts and hands as we sing hallelujah to God-Goddess, for we are so blessed to have incarnated at this most important and precious time on earth. It is here, even though the old ways will be hanging around for a bit. The new has been successfully birthed and is being cared for while The Divine Feminine grows stronger each day with all our love. Love is the force. Love is the action. Love is a noun and a verb. Love is what is real. "All you need is love!" The Beatles gave us that song back in the sixties.

Look into your heart. What brings you alive? Passion? Joy? What makes your heart smile? Follow that love, that joy, that bliss. That is your roadmap.

This book weaves a story of my life. It tells of the ways I was shut down. All the ways I was hypnotized into believing I wasn't good, wasn't enough, was bad. Something was wrong with me.

But the truth is, we aren't the bad things that happened to us. They were part of the fray of the time in which we were living in. Falsity, lies, power. Power over others. The roar of it was sickening. Trampling indigenous values and villages for oil, for money. Believing some lives didn't matter. To many, money was more important than the heart or the soul of all humanity.

Now a new vibration is penetrating the earth, bringing truth to the forefront; love and kindness, we, not they, together not isolated, goodness, not evil, wholeness, not fragmentation. A new dream is materializing before our very eyes here on Planet Earth. Signs of the times like the white lions of Africa and their connection to the sun and to God-Goddess. Shamans and truth. Miracles abound!

But you won't find this on the news. The news is a boombox designed to keep you in fear and survival mode. Fear, bad things, murders, are bombarded continuously into your consciousness. We are told to stay in fear and don't open your eyes to love.

Love, joy, unity, and wellness are our tickets to the new paradigm.

Women throughout the ages have had sex forced upon them by fathers, grandfathers, brothers, friends of the family. On a trip I led to the Amazon rainforest a girlfriend, while on an ayuhuasca journey working with a shaman, experienced her older brother throwing a blanket over them both and having sex with her when she was a very young child. She had repressed the memory, but it showed up on the sacred journey.

I also had many incidents of sexual molestation perpetrated on me for years and years. I could see each incident, and I had to keep vomiting it up and vomiting it out to cleanse myself while I was working with the shaman as well. It also came out in hypnosis and working with a trauma therapist. My traumas didn't live in my conscious memories. I had to leave my body every time the sexual molestations happened as a child. I loved and I hated my father. I loved how he could make us laugh and how absolutely fun he could be. I hated that he hurt us.

I have a friend whose father was a priest in England. He and other men from the church raped her so often it damaged her young body. Now as a grown woman, she is unable to bear children.

I can't believe what so many of my girlfriends and I and women everywhere, have gone through, had to endure. One day I realized I am not the bad things that have happened to me. I am, we are, of the Light, and this cannot be stolen from us by anyone. My light is my God-Goddess given sovereign right. I am, we are, innately good. I am good. We are good. No matter all the lies we have been told and sold. We are goodness incarnate. We can't be stained, tainted, or defiled. We are and always will be whole and complete. This is who I am and who we are. We are courageous and we cannot be swayed.

In the 1950's, for the most part, women in America didn't work. They were housewives being held hostage by men because the man held the financial power in the house. Women were secondary and didn't have a voice. Women didn't want the embarrassment of what the neighbors and others would think. By not working, not having a paying job, women were tethered to their husbands, who held the power. Women lost their voice and gave away their power.

The feminine being who is in her power has dominion over her sexuality. This can manifest as an enjoyment of pleasurable sex, and she says who can come in and who stays out. She is sovereign and uses her wisdom and knowing within her body to guide her moment to moment to her deepest truth. The feminine, claiming her power, follows her body's feelings. She is no longer tied to thoughts of what others think about her. She is concerned with what is real, not image.

The molestation of sex from fathers, brothers, uncles, neighbors, and priests retains power over her. She believes she is the bad thing that has happened to her. She believes she is bad. She shuts down. Her self-worth is diminished, believing she deserves to be punished. Once sovereign, though, she knows this is not true. She knows she is innately good, and that can't be taken away from her by others.

The fierce feminine tells the truth without blame or judgment. She has the courage for terrible things to be seen, not hidden. She is a truth-teller. She doesn't care what others think. She isn't concerned with image but what is true. She follows her heart, her body wisdom, her feelings, and inner knowing. She can communicate her feelings in a direct way without blame or judgment. It took me many years to understand and embody these concepts. I was able to be in my power in the outer world of business and appearances, but it took me living through a challenging marriage to truly see how I hadn't developed my inner power and my fierce feminine self.

As I write this book, I am sitting at my large dining-room table, looking out the sliding glass doors at the surrounding red rock mountains of Sedona, that I love so dearly. Sugarloaf, the heart chakra mountain of Sedona lives at the base of my front door and Thunder Mountain is right next to it. It is one of three spots where the root chakra of the entire world resides. It is a very powerful place to live.

The chakras reside within us and on the earth. They are energy centers. When they are aligned with our higher purpose, we are in the flow of our sacred life. When they are out of alignment, we feel disconnected and fragmented. As I write this book, I am held in deep gratitude, knowing I am supported by the root and heart chakras as I reveal the most intimate and vulnerable aspects of my life to you.

I begin our journey with my challenging marriage to show how I gave my power away and then learned how to regain it.

CHAPTER THREE

LOSING MY POWER

I was doing what I dreamed by pursuing a career in fashion, which I could not have done living in Utah. I was working for Levi Strauss in Los Angeles and I was named Levi "Sales Representative of the Year," for the Los Angeles Region, when the salesforce was 90% men. I barely weighed 100 pounds, and I was very pretty. My regional manager felt that women needed to be a bull in a china shop to succeed. But I took care and loved my clients who were the owners of stores I served. I would ask myself, "If this was my store, what does it need to be successful?" I would present my ideas and they would love them, and this brought them greater sales. I loved my clients, and they loved me. My energy was on fire.

It was MAGIC time (Men's Apparel Guild in California) and I was at a five-day event that would be held a couple times a year to debut new lines from trendy clothing brands for retail stores. It was business during the day and partying hard at night. It was a time of little sleep. I loved my job. I had been rookie of the year, and then the following year the Sales Representative of the year for our Region. My territory was in Southern California servicing the areas between

San Bernardino and Anaheim. I needed to live in my territory, and my manager placed me in the town of Brea, about a half hour from the beaches.

I lived in an apartment complex. I had come home from the MAGIC show exhausted from the work and partying late each night and had fallen asleep in my bed. My girlfriend, Paula, in the apartment across from me, kept calling, "Kathleen, I have the man for you!" I told her, "I don't care if he's Prince Charming!" I was in bed sleeping after being on the go non-stop for the past week. My phone rang again. It was Paula, "Do you have some ice I can borrow?" "Yes, I need to bring the samples in from my car. I'll meet you on the sidewalk." I jumped into a pair of jeans and a tee shirt, no bra or makeup or even shoes, to deliver a bag of ice. I met Richard on the sidewalk instead of Paula. "Come to the party," he said. I said "No," and he said, "I am not going to take no for an answer!"

I was intrigued because none of my peers talked to me like that. I changed my clothes, put on some lipstick and went to the party. We talked to each other with such ease. He was fascinating and funny, and I could tell he was highly intelligent, with unbound confidence. He walked me to my door and kissed me lightly on my lips as we said good-bye.

Just two days later, my telephone rang in the morning and I wondered who would be calling that early. "Hi, it's Richard from the party, and I was wondering if we could have a date Saturday night?" I replied "It's a really busy time for me as the new samples have just come out. I don't have time to date now but when things slow down, I will give you a call." Richard was stunned. This was a first for him, being turned down for a date. There was a joke at his workplace that his secretary was the most popular person in the entire company as all the eligible women took her to lunch hoping to get to him through her. Women even sent him flowers. So he was totally taken aback and stunned by my rejection.

A few weeks later I was invited to a black-tie party at a fancy hotel to watch the Academy Awards. I called and asked Richard if he would like to be my date. After several seconds he replied, "I am so sorry to turn you down, but I have been invited to the real Academy Awards and won't be able to attend your little party." And then he added, "But how soon can we have our first date?"

Our first date was April 1st, which was the date I had set an intention to meet the man I would marry. We went to dinner at an intimate ethnic restaurant in a quaint neighborhood. I was so tired of the lackluster chain restaurants where most guys would take me to eat and dance.

After dinner he took me to his small house he rented which was right on the beach. He wrapped me in a wool blanket he had brought back from some faraway place on one of his many travels around the world. The warm ocean breeze caressed our bodies as the coolness of the night hovered. We snuggled and made out under the stars while listening to the pulse of Grandmother Ocean. We moved inside and were still kissing on his bed when he murmured, "Our children are going to be so beautiful." Right then the telephone rang, and he went into the bathroom to talk for an extended time. He came back saying it was an old girlfriend in a crisis. I would later find out it was his girlfriend who lived in the Bay Area with whom he was in a long-term relationship when he met me. He drove to the Bay Area to break up with her.

We had exciting dates like skydiving where I was the only woman, and all the men were taking bets on who would get closest to the target and ignored me because I was female. But I was the one who nearly landed on the target and all the men were literally out in the cow pastures.

Much later we went snow skiing together. We were on a difficult black-diamond run, and as we came to a gigantic cornice of pure ice Richard turned to me to ask what I thought about the run, but I was already half way down the mountain.

When Richard and I first got together, he witnessed me heal a horse that had fallen off of a huge cliff to the ground. All the surrounding people were crying out that it was dead. I connected to the Divine, and exactly as I saw it in my mind's eye, while connecting to God-Goddess, I envisioned the horse healed. The horse jumped up, and words were exclaimed by the people, "What a miracle. Look, the horse is alive!"

We had been dating for five months when I had a sales meeting in Hawaii. Richard said, "Let's go early, and bring a white dress, just in case." We told our parents that we would probably get married there. We did not know what complications were involved and his mother had a couple of stipulations: 1. Get married by someone from a church. 2. Have a professional photographer take photos. We also found out we needed blood tests. The blood tests were easy; they could be done straight away and the results were fast. Now it was time to find a reverend and a professional photographer. The woman, helping answer our questions, told us her best friend on the Big Island was a reverend and she was sure he would marry us. She then said "I am a professional photographer. Would you like me to take photos for you?" It felt like the Divine had orchestrated everything for us. As I was slipping into my white dress, I glanced over at Richard who had just downed his second scotch. This was not like him! We were married on the shores of the ocean in the early evening. The next morning, we went hiking on a volcano. Richard had laryngitis and could barely talk by that evening; and he was covered in hives.

As we were leaving the condominium we had rented, I asked if he had $15 to leave a tip for the housekeeper. He put a few dollars and some change on the table, and I said, "That's not enough money!" With that, he shoved me forcefully into the wall and said, "Don't you ever call me a liar again!" I was in shock. Later I was wondering if I should get my marriage annulled. We parted, me to my sales meeting in Oahu, and Richard back to California. It would be a week before I saw or talked to him again. I was planning to get a taxi at the airport when Richard met me with a diamond and ruby wedding ring, a dozen red roses and a bottle of champagne asking me, "Can you forgive me? Can we start over again?"

In retrospect, I realize Richard never drank hard liquor during the day either before or after we were married. He occasionally had a glass of wine with dinner or a scotch before dinner if we were out with friends. He was using alcohol to cover up what he couldn't admit or totally feel and communicate. And the laryngitis and hives were his body's response to his unspoken emotions. If I had this knowledge when he said "Can we start over?" I would have followed through by annulling our marriage or made a condition of us getting therapy to work on why he would be so cruel and have such a strong reaction to us getting married. Instead, I overrode my concern and listened to others' advice. I also felt loved and adored by him when he came with a dozen red roses and a diamond and ruby wedding ring. I was swept off my feet. And gave up my power.

When we were newly married, we loved to drive up the coast of California and get out of the city into nature. We were visiting Mendocino for a long weekend together and we fell in love with a parcel of land we later bought, even though the interest rates were extremely high at that time. On one such trip, just after purchasing the land, we were enjoying a picnic and the view. Richard shared a traumatic event that happened when he was a young child. He told me his father had worked hard earning money for their very first home. On their first visit with the whole family to the house, his father was showing everyone around and went to turn on the light in the basement which wasn't turning on, so he lit a match. There had been a significant gas leak, and the whole house exploded off the foundation into flames. They were all on fire. Richard, who was three years old at the time, was rolled in gravel to put out the flames. The doctors thought Richard would be blind, but he regained his eyesight. Richard's mother and father were taken to different hospitals.

When Richards's dad was in the hospital and heavily sedated, the gas company went to him and had him sign papers releasing the company from any liability. Adele, his mother, who was pregnant when the house exploded, suffered the least. A local witch told Adele, "Your baby is going to be born with a mark from this fire," Richards's brother Gavin was born a while later, a healthy baby. I remember Richard mentioning that Gavin was born with a mark, just like the witch stated.

He went on to tell me about his younger brother and two best friends. Richard was living in Colorado shortly after college, and his brother, Gavin, was on his way to visit him, hitchhiking from Oklahoma when a young woman in a Volkswagen van picked him up. She lost control of the van, and the crash was so bad they both died immediately. Richard was called by the morgue to identify his brother. He had to call his parents to tell them their youngest son was dead. Gavin's head was severed in the crash. At the moment of his death, the wooden clock Gavin had given his mother as a gift stopped telling time. Gavin's favorite flowers were peonies. His parents planted a peony bush at his grave, It finally bloomed several decades later when his father died and was buried next to Gavin.

A couple of months after Gavin's death, two of Richard's close friends also had a similar car wreck on the mountain roads of Colorado. After all of this trauma, Richard packed his bags and traveled for a while, ending up in Fiji. When he returned, he went back to school and got a master's degree in international business and finance. That degree propelled him into his successful career.

I remember when the company that Richard worked for was bidding on a job bigger than they had ever bid on before. He told me it would be impossible to win it. I told him it would be impossible to win it with that attitude. I asked him if he wanted to win it. Each evening, I would have him lie down on the sofa and I would go through visioning and him using his five senses; smelling, tasting, hearing, seeing and touch as well as feeling what winning this big job would be like. Richard took all this visioning to his office and trained his team to do it with him.

Not too much later, Richard's team won this job, and it put Richard on his successful career trajectory. He got a promotion and was transferred to London. This meant I ended up leaving my career with Levi Strauss and following him. Before he won the big job, I was making more money than he was.

Richard moved to London first, and I stayed behind to get things finished with my career before handing it over to another sales representative. Richard had sold his car, I still needed to sell mine, and I had numerous other details to attend to. I needed to go to Salt Lake City to say good-bye to my family as well as drop off Paco, Richard's green parrot. My sweet sister Patti had agreed to take care of Paco while we were gone. Richard asked if I would stop by Oklahoma and meet his parents on my way. It was the middle of winter and snowing hard in Oklahoma when I arrived. I arrived at his parents' home with seven suitcases in preparation for my new life in London. The following day it was snowing lightly as his mother took me to her workplace, where she was a manager of a Hallmark store and dress shop. It was fun seeing where she worked and meeting her co-workers and friends. We left and the light snow had turned into a blizzard over a couple of hours. In a moment of thinking about Richard, I glanced at my wedding ring of rubies and a diamond in the center. Where the diamond should be was very dark. In fact, it was not there! I started visioning with my five senses for the diamond being found. That night as we were sitting down for dinner the telephone rang. It was Adele's assistant saying, "we were just vacuuming, and my boyfriend came to get me and said, "stop what's that sparkling?" She responded "It is Kathleen's diamond!" Thank you, God-Goddess, for another miracle!

Richard had called while I was visiting with his parents and found out that I had seven suitcases. I got it down to six. You were only allowed two free bags on the plane and each one after that had a charge. So, this was going to cost money. He wasn't happy; in fact, he was furious and berated me for being so naive. When I got to the airline, they said there's going to be a charge for each extra suitcase. I told the agent at the counter, "I've never traveled overseas so I didn't know about this rule, but I can tell you I'll never make this mistake again. I am flying to London for my first time to meet my husband. We were recently married and then he got transferred!" The agent stepped away and returned with his boss saying, "We have a wedding present for you. There will be no charges on your extra luggage."

It was the early eighties in London, and it was a rundown city. People seemed dour. No one looked at me and no one smiled. I would pinch myself to see if I had become an invisible ghost, because no one ever acknowledged me. I did not feel seen. I was lonely. I had gone from tons of friends and being popular, and had been asked to marry more than 20 times, to a husband who was more interested in his career and being successful than in me. Richard had his work. I didn't have mine.

I made nice meals and kept the flat clean. He told me if I were bored, I should be spending time at the British Museum and Tower of

London. But the Tower creeped me out. Must have been past lives! When Richard would open the door to our apartment I would run and jump up on him and wrap my legs around his waist and give him a huge kiss. Because of this he nicknamed me Monkey. Later, when I stopped drinking alcohol, my nickname was shortened to Monk, as he said I lived like one.

Richard told me we didn't have two incomes, only his. So now, he put me on a budget. I wasn't given money for clothing, and I had to account for every penny I spent. I felt like I had been tossed into the Tower of London and the key thrown away! Even though we were struggling, we held onto our land in Mendocino which we were making monthly payments on. We intended to build on it and to retire there.

I was used to living in sunny Southern California where everyone was smiling and would say "Hi." Now I no longer had a car and had to walk in the cold and pouring rain three blocks to get to the Tube. It was dreary. The people felt dreary. There was no eye contact, no smiles. It was my first time as an adult experiencing a dark night of the soul. I no longer had a career and I had worked in one way or another since the age of ten babysitting, and when I could, I started working at a real job at the age of sixteen.

One evening Richard and I went out to a watch a stage play and have an early dinner. We got off the Tube after this lovely evening, and I looked down at my wrist to see only two of my three bangles. I had lost a 22-carat bangle Richard had gifted me shortly after we had gotten married. He had purchased them many years prior when he was working in Saudi Arabia. It was winter and I was dressed in a long wool winter coat with a warm scarf around my neck and leather gloves. We had made it to the street above when I noticed it missing, and I immediately started to vision with my five senses in order to find the missing bangle. We went back down to the Tube platform where a janitor was sweeping the floor, and I spotted something sparkling right in front of him. I ran and grabbed the bangle from the pile he had swept up. What a miracle that so many people had passed by the bangle and not seen it. I was again using the power of visualization and imagination to protect and find my lost bracelet. My diamond had been found, and now this bangle.

Shortly after moving to London, Richard had a business trip to Egypt and I went with him. One morning after he went off to work, I was in the hotel lobby and ran into a man who told me he was a professor of ancient archaeology. His tour group had just been canceled. He said he would give me a private tour for the price of a group tour. I said, "Oh my goodness, this is my lucky day. I have always been so fascinated by Egypt!" He took me to a few sacred sites, but also to the place where Saint Laurent would purchase essential oils for their signature perfumes. I bought a few of these oils. Then we went to a store that had beautiful gems at a fraction of the price in the western world. I thought I bought genuine stones of emerald, ruby and sapphire, but apparently I had not. I gave the professor a large tip for such a magical wonderful day. Then he said, "Tomorrow, if you meet someone, and they say they are a professor of ancient archaeology, don't go with this person." That felt like a strange thing to say I thought as I walked away.

Richard greeted me saying, "What do you have in that bag?" I showed him and he asked, "How much did you spend?" I replied "Two-hundred dollars." In an angry voice Richard said, "I can't believe I married you. You are so fucking naïve to be scammed. I don't know how I can stay married to a person like you."

I replied, "I will get all the money back!" Richard retorted, "This isn't Saks Fifth Avenue, you will never see a penny of that money again" and he walked out of our room, closed the door and didn't come back all night. The next morning, I got my shopping bag and went to the doorman asking him to arrange a taxi. I was crying and said my husband wanted to divorce me because the professor had defrauded me the day before and I needed to return these items.

A taxi pulled up to our hotel, and I was able to tell him where to go for the essential oils I had purchased the day before. It turned out the hotel doorman had told the Professor I was crying and my husband wanted to divorce me. He found me in the first shop we had gone to the previous day and said, "Please, I will take you to each place and we will get all of your money back." Oh, what a miracle! In fact, I was given a gift of one of the essential oils to keep.

I left all the torn-up receipts in an ashtray from the day before with a note for Richard to meet me by the pool and I had gotten all the money back that I had spent. Once again, I had made the impossible, possible.

Richard was often traveling five days a week with his job. I loved my quiet time alone in our flat and dreaded the weekends when he would come home, and everything would be life according to him. I stayed married. We thought having a baby would help our marriage, and we both really wanted a baby with all our hearts. I got pregnant immediately. We were both happy and thrilled. I went from weighing 105 pounds to 150 pounds. I looked thin from the back, but from the side I was huge, and people who would never even glance at me before would rubber-neck as I walked by.

We had the hardest time coming up with a name for a boy that we both liked. I would suggest a name and Richard would say "No, that was the name of the imbecile in my school." No matter what name one of us would produce there was always a reason the other one didn't like it. We could not agree on a name for our baby boy who was arriving very soon. We couldn't come to an agreement until one day we drove by the Big Ben Clock Tower, and I said, "I feel like I have BIG BEN in my belly!" Aha, the name for our baby had landed. Ben was such a sweet, intelligent, kind, and curious baby. We both absolutely adored him.

When I was pregnant with Ben, my neonatal doctor had ordered some tests to be run. When they came back it looked as if Ben's spine wasn't forming properly, and the doctor told me he would be born with a deformity. Every single day after that I envisioned Ben being a healthy and well child, perfect in every way. When he was born the doctor was very surprised because he expected Ben to be abnormal. He looked him over carefully and declared Ben to be perfect.

Shortly after his birth, we were invited to stay in a beautiful home across from Hyde Park. The owners, our friends, had to leave the country because of a lawsuit. They had a couple of stipulations placed on us: we needed to keep the housekeeper and care for their cat, Sylvester. Are you kidding? I was in seventh heaven! Now I had a beautiful home, a housekeeper three times a week, and we would also get their BMW luxury sedan to drive. There were beautiful trees, shops, and art galleries within walking distance, and even if Richard had me on a budget, it didn't really matter. We no longer had to pay rent, which actually is typical for the company to do for an employee living in a foreign country.

We soon began meeting wonderful friends both English, and other ex-pats like us. Additionally, I met a woman at the baby clinic who was Swedish and had lived and worked in New York City. We became dear friends. We were having such a fantastic time living there. Things finally started to look up for me.

We had been to Paris for a reunion of Richard's international graduate school. Even though Richard had me on a strict budget, which didn't include new clothes, I stumbled upon a beautiful, inexpensive evening dress. It was made of black velvet with gathered black satin in the middle of it and had a big velvet bow at the waist and puffy black velvet sleeves a few inches above the elbow. The neck was cut low in a straight line. It looked like something out of Vogue, and Richard had actually bought it for me.

One evening Richard came home from work and told me we were going to a concert and after that we would be with a small group of people who would be meeting Princess Diana, the patron of this event. All day I rehearsed the proper words to say to a Princess.

When we arrived, it was not the intimate event Richard had been told but we were in a ballroom filled with at least 150 people or more. Richard said he would take our coats and get them checked. I was waiting for him at the entrance of the ballroom, and when I looked up, Princess Diana was about ten feet in front of me. Our eyes briefly met as she looked up at me as she was in a conversation with some people.

Richard returned, and we were walking around socializing with people, when a man approached me directly and said that Princess Diana had chosen three people she wanted to meet and talk to that evening, and I was one of them. Would I like to meet her? I replied "Yes!" and asked if my husband could also meet her, and he said "Yes." So that evening we had the most fortunate opportunity to meet Princess Diana and have a lovely conversation with her. I remember her beautiful, big eyes and eyelashes and how she was kind of shy, how she would say something and then look downward. I asked her about her recent trip to the USA, and she mentioned Prince Charles was home taping the show *Dynasty* for her.

In the span of 22 years Richard transferred from London to Scotland, to Istanbul, to Los Angeles, to San Francisco, to Bethesda, Maryland, to Mill Valley, California, to London again and back to California.

We moved from London to Scotland on Ben's first birthday. Everyone in Scotland was so sweet, kind, and friendly. We lived in a rural area, which was such a refreshing change. Everyone in the countryside would stop what they were doing to help us with the "wee one," unlike London, where sometimes we would be invisible.

Richard was transferred to Istanbul when Ben was 18 months old. Richard and I were a little terrified because the film *Midnight Express* had recently come out, and we had this image of it being dangerous to live in Istanbul. But we moved there and found the opposite to be true. We found an apartment where one of the wealthiest men in Turkey had a penthouse and guards. That made us feel safe. The apartment had good bones, but an ugly old carpet. I found I could roll it up and store it until we left, and it turned into a stunning place. It had beautiful hardwood floors. The apartment wasn't big, but it wasn't small either. In the back was grass and the front of our apartment had a balcony and deck and the most magnificent views of the Bosphorus Strait right below us. And when we originally looked at the apartment, they had one stipulation: keep the housekeeper who worked there five days a week.

The people in Istanbul were the friendliest I have ever met anywhere. Even teenage boys would stop and stoop down and stroke Ben's cheek with two fingers saying, "*choke gazelle*," which means 'very beautiful' in Turkish. I could have lived there for the rest of my life. I loved the weather, the beauty, the people, the ancient museums, and the incredible sites to visit like Cappadocia. Unfortunately, we were only there for six months before Richard was needed back in the USA. Suddenly our international salary was drastically cut. We moved to a dull suburb in Southern California.

Ben was just two years old and so curious, perceptive, and thoughtful. Richard was traveling during the week but home on the weekends. Life was so quiet with Ben and me. I read to him and took him to the park to play. He had a ton of Legos and he loved to build and create.

When Richard was home on the weekends the house would explode with the rumble-tumble fun that only a father and son can share.

Ben was in preschool. Once again, I had a strict budget, no housekeeper or any help. We had to buy two cars and I found used ones. I got my real estate license and was excited to go back to work.

Richard was transferred to San Francisco when Ben turned four, and I interviewed with the top real estate companies in the Pacific Heights area. They all wanted me. I chose the one I liked best. After two sales of extremely expensive homes and my lucrative commissions Richard told me I had to stop working, that my hours were unpredictable and he wanted me at home full time. So once again, all the fun and love I had of meeting people, making money, and enjoying myself came to an end.

I still wanted to work, so I took a job as the manager of a store called the *Ark* next to the Waldorf school where Ben was attending. I worked while he was in school. The store carried books and toys in line with the philosophy of the Waldorf educational system. Richard loved playing and having fun with Ben but didn't want anything to interrupt their time. He wanted me there to serve and meet all his own needs, which I did in spades. Socializing, having dinner parties, playing the corporate wife role and completely taking care of everything was my job. I found myself in a similar role as a caretaker that my mother had with my father.

Many years later I was going on a road trip. I had stumbled upon Angeles Arrien's six cassette tape deck called "The Second Half of

Life." Angeles taught that if you find the courage to change at midlife, a miracle happens. Your character is opened, deepened, strengthened, and softened. You return to your soul's highest values. You are now prepared to create your legacy, an imprint of your dream for our world, a dream that can fully come true in the second half of life. She is also the author of the book *The Four Fold Way*.

After listening to all six cassette tapes, I fell in love with her work. I looked on the back to find more information about her and there was a telephone number. I called, a woman answered and said Angeles Arrien had a year-long program beginning that week in Sausalito; there was one spot left, would I like it. We were living in Mill Valley just a few minutes away. I replied "YES!" That was in February, 1999. I was a student of hers for three years including summer vision quests.

One of my greatest takeaways from studying with her was to always listen to your heart and follow it. Doing anything from "duty" was dead. It had no life force. I realized my role of a corporate wife held no juice for me. It was totally done from duty and what I was expected to do. Now I made a commitment to only do what lit up my heart, what I truly loved.

That spring, Angeles Arrien led our group on a shamanic drumming journey where the beat of a drum at a certain rhythm takes you into another reality. You can set an intention beforehand as to what you want to focus on. On this journey I asked about my marriage. I saw the bright blue summer sky and then clouds appeared spelling D-I-V-O-R-C-E, each letter was one cloud. I was shown that Richard and I came together to create our son, and once that was fulfilled, I would be set free from him to do the work I had come into the world to do.

Later in the summer of 1999, I went on my first vision quest, a three-day journey into remote nature. Each participant is told to find their own individual spot to set up camp. We would fast on water, lemon juice, cayenne pepper, and a small amount of maple syrup. Then we partnered up with another person in the group, staying silent the entire time. We could only signal to each other in the mornings, at a specific time and place to check in and make sure we were okay. We each set an intention for the vision quest. On one of the evenings, I had a powerful nighttime dream. I am lost in a train station, I cannot find my way out and it is underground. I am being followed by women from the company my husband works for. I see something and think it's my purse but as I get closer, I see that it's a man's briefcase. A man picks up the briefcase and walks away. I find my purse and empty the contents of my purse into the garbage bin nearby. In the bin, I find presents that are wrapped, so I put them into my purse.

I wake and come to an understanding of the significance of the dream. I was following the masculine world, and by throwing out the contents of my purse, I was throwing away and disowning my deepest feminine essence, emptying out what was no longer needed and retrieving my gifts. Gifts that I would later realize.

During this time, I found a woman in Mill Valley named Pilar, who taught voice lessons and said she could teach anyone to sing on key. She had worked with hundreds of clients. It was the beginning of me wanting to reclaim my voice. At that time I was still unaware of my traumas which had yet to surface, but this would be the spearhead of that journey. It was the beginning of my opening in so many ways. My heart, voice, and sovereignty were starting to take shape and beginning to bloom. At first, I was so frozen I could not sing at all. But with Pilar's love and belief in me, I was finally able to sing on key! She was celebrating her birthday with a large house party and had invited me, but not Richard. She only invited friends of her heart to her party. This was such a new concept to me, but it was also totally in line with the teachings I was learning from Angeles Arrien. Only do things from your heart and not from a place of "duty."

Richard's career continued to soar while we were living in Mill Valley. He became a partner, and over the years he would become president of the company and later a director.

One day while we were living in Mill Valley and Ben was still in grade school, Richard said he thought it would be easier for me to have a local bank account that would be mine for paying all the bills and household items. He would deposit money into it from his bank account that I didn't have access to. At some point, he didn't seem as interested and had started to relax regarding my budget. I bought a beautiful handmade silver bracelet in a store in downtown Mill Valley, and he never said anything. My clothing budget was starting to loosen. I would sign my name on income tax papers without looking at them as he was running out the door to work, and we never discussed money anymore. I was so relieved when I finally didn't have a budget and have to account for every dollar I spent. I now see how this was another way I gave my power away. I chose to remain ignorant about our financial situation and accept it the way he had set it up.

Richard was transferred back to London in Ben's junior year of high school in 2001 for a more prominent position than he had ever held in his career. I wondered why I hated being the President's wife, which came with a number of duties. I was expected to hold afternoon coffees and afternoon entertainment for the wives. When I checked into my heart, it was screaming, "No!" Some people relished it, but I despised the fakery and performance that being a corporate wife demanded. I was hiding behind Richard. I was not coming forward in my truest essence. The power in our relationship was Richard's, not mine. I was an accessory to him in the relationship, an afterthought to help him look good. I wanted something real, and I knew that Richard was never going to see ME. It also felt like I was supposed to be static, not fluid, not alive, and not moving. It felt stifling, and suffocating, and I was stuck in a freaking role! There was an expectation of what a corporate wife was, and I was definitely not that any longer.

I wasn't interested in standing around talking about all our latest vacations and other small talk. I wanted to do something that had heart and meaning for me. Luckily, there was a woman there who was already doing the coffees. Her husband had been an ambassador to two different countries in Europe, and this was the life she loved. I offered to design and lead a course from the chapters of the book *The Artists Way* about creativity. We would gather around my large dining-room table sharing hopes, emotional vulnerabilities, being real and living our truth. We came together once a week to share our newly found creativity and everyone loved the class. We were all growing together. I loved producing fun things to do in conjunction with each chapter. Now I was living a life from my heart and not one from duty. I still hear from a few of the women who were in the class with me, and I am so grateful to everyone who attended. I think it was this class that planted the seeds of me leading women in creativity and self-growth later on in my life. I had daydreams of sharing rituals with women that would show up in my consciousness. I had pictures of seeing myself teaching, and leading different things.

During this time, I took an all-day writing workshop and this is the piece I created that day:

MY ANCESTORS

"Release the fear; recognize your own worth and power."
These were the words I drew from the Ancestor cards.
Little black words on a small white card, but how powerful and true.
My sisters were visiting. I brought them over to London for a week.

Something was gnawing at me – that which I couldn't put my finger on?
Beautiful, smart, and talented, but we don't KNOW it.
The fear that holds us back from being truly great and powerful.
Fear in our bones.
Bones that break on both sides of my ancestors.
Granny's back broken in so many places.
My mother's hip and her arm.

Our lives resemble weather patterns like volcanoes and hurricanes.
The excitement of something major always going on, even if it isn't good weather.
Not a balmy day with palm trees swaying and gentle breezes caressing their leaves.
But, gales of wind that rip plants and trees out from the earth and toss them like a blade of grass.

The laughter and wit and charm can turn upside down.
The FEAR.
All that beautiful talent and brains stifled,
Too afraid to move to do something wrong, make a mistake.
Staying still, the only safe way to survive.
Still, don't move, a hunter may shoot you.
Don't be heard, don't be seen,
You will be safe and survive just like the animals in nature.
Camouflage, blend into the environment and it will keep you alive.
Break the chain of fear.
Recognize our worth and power.

Oh Ancestors, what you have gone through.
All that beauty, talent, brains, wit, and charm
forever sunk deep into the bowels of the earth.
Where it can't be seen.
Where light can't penetrate.

Somehow the light shines through and
Touches, something stirs and is alive and moving.
The gifts of intuition, the seers from the generations
Are awakened and alive,
Stepping forth.

The light blots out the darkness.
The fear is overcome with the light.
The light always prevails.

Not hiding behind someone else.
Willing to step up and say,
"Hey, this is MY POWER, IS MY GOD-GIVEN BIRTHRIGHT,
AND I ACCEPT IT."
I live in the Light in my power.
I accept who I am and my destiny.

I will go forward.
I am ready to go forward to release the chains that have held my ancestors down for so many years.
Break the chain.
Break the chain.
Don't I hear those words softly rolling around all of the time in my head?

Life on earth was so harsh and unpredictable.
I tried to be such a good girl to do everything right.
Don't make a mistake.
I learned it's not okay to make a mistake.
I had to do everything just right.
Never make a mistake.
Mistakes mean pain and punishment at home, and humiliation at school.

I lived in a straitjacket of fear.
Try to be perfect, to be good and to do what's right.
Babysit your sisters and brother.
Don't ask for anything from anyone, and maybe, just maybe, I could be loved.

If I got small enough,
Insignificant enough,
Didn't have a voice and was responsible and helpful to everyone.
Be a good girl. Maybe, just maybe, I will find love.

By Kathleen Plant Lov

All of my exploration with my voice, with writing and the vision quests I had gone on, gave me a deeper connection to my heart and soul and my creativity. I was starting to find my lost self. I had reached a point that I could no longer tolerate Richard's tone of voice to me and his demeaning actions and expectations. I chose to move out of our bedroom to a room on another floor of our home in Belgravia, London. I saw a therapist as well as a healer. I finally got the courage to ask for a divorce. On the day I was going to ask Richard for a divorce, I got a phone call. It was Richard's mother saying that Richard's father had just died. Now I felt I couldn't ask him for a divorce. I needed to be there to support him through this difficult time. I felt it was the wrong time to leave Richard.

CHAPTER FOUR

CAMINO DE SANTIAGO

After returning from Richard's father's funeral it was clear to me I could not turn back. The new connection to myself and my need for sovereignty was now my north star. I was called to walk the Camino de Santiago. My intention for walking the Camino was walking away from my life as a corporate wife into my deepest, truest self, into a life with heart and meaning. One that lit me up and brought me into my most authentic self. Walking this sacred journey away from my old life into a new one that would be revealed to me in Divine Perfect Timing.

It was the Camino de Santiago trip that helped me witness my stamina, courage, and strength along with the ability to walk 480 miles alone in Southern France into the Spanish mountains and countryside. Just turning fifty. In the beginning of the trip, I had planned everything, being careful of the weight I was carrying. The total weight was under 12 pounds, but I made the mistake of buying new hiking boots without breaking them in first. This detail, on a journey for me that involved 35 days of consistent walking, was a small oversight to say the least. I had to stop for a solid three days to nurse bone spurs and blisters. Fortunately, there were many kind pilgrims, as they are called, who passed by with homeopathic remedies, thick Band-aids and salves, good stories, and some laughs over food. On the third day of nursing my feet back into hobbling condition, I used my handmade walking stick, which I purchased from a gentleman selling walking sticks along the path when I first set out. I refitted my boots with sheepskin and wrapped duct tape around my feet to cover the blisters. I set back out. I was being pushed — like an invisible force guiding me toward my next step along the path.

The journey itself was profound. It's known for the spiritual transformations that people go through. For me, it was planting seeds for big changes that were going to take place in my life. I was letting go of the old Kathleen and being led by spirit to my new beginnings.

Fortunately, once up and hobbling along the path again, I managed to arrive at the Church of San Juan in perfect timing for the Autumn equinox. It is the only time in the cycle of the year which the setting sun perfectly illuminates the face of the statue Mother Mary at sunset. I had no idea! I was approached by a woman named Nancy who exclaimed, "You have arrived at the perfect time!" We went together inside the church for this sacred moment in time holding hands and crying as we witnessed what felt like Mary coming to life as the light of the setting sun illuminated her. Afterward we went to the courtyard where I was anointed with spikenard, the same essential oil that was said to have been used to anoint Jesus' head prior to crucifixion. Nancy anointed me on my forehead and initiated me into the Divine Feminine Mysteries.

I felt so safe walking the Camino. There were many churches, and *refugios* available to rest or stay in. I met many amazing people along the way. Straight off, I met a woman and her husband. She had just been cured of cancer and wanted to do this journey because she realized how fragile life truly is. I also met a young man who was walking with a German Shepherd he found along the path. We walked together for a few days, shared *refugio*, profound conversations and laughter. I met others with whom I also walked and found quaint restaurants in small towns and villages along the way.

This pilgrimage set the tone for monumental changes in my world that were yet to come. Honestly, I had no clue that my life was going to take the direction it has.

A PILGRIM AND HER BACKPACK

Exchanging hiking boots
four times.
Afternoon before trip
Small outdoor store in London
Finally finding YOU!!
Third time a charm!
Slightly larger than a day pack
Blue and grey Berghaus
Two side pockets
Two on top flap
Secret one inside

Scales on kitchen floor
Weighing every item...
Three pairs black underpants
Small but not sexy
Three pairs wool socks
Red flip flops
Two lightweight hiking pants
Zippers turning them to shorts.
Three tee shirts, but no bra
Long sleeved button-down cotton shirt
Northface vest
GORE-TEX rain gear,
Pants and jacket folding into their pockets.
Floppy hat, Ray Ban sunglasses
Sleeping bag (three bought before finding lightest)
Travel towel – gift from friends
Scissored in half to save space
Scarf designed to wear 6 ways
4 large safety pins turning back pack to
instant clothesline!
As clothes need washing daily.
Camelback
Canteen with duct tape wound around it
Hair cropped short, manicure and pedicure -what the heck
Mini everything...
Shampoo, deodorant stick broken off in baggie
Soap for body and clothes, toothbrush, and paste
Sunblock, razor and Chapstick
Earplugs—
Godsend in refugios,
Three mesh ditty bags

KATHLEEN PLANT LOV

Band-aids, needle, and thread for blisters
Medicinal ice patches, arnica, rhus tox and joint vitamins
Tiny Swiss army knife, mini mag lite head lamp — too heavy,
left behind
Tiny Dictaphone but no camera,
Desire to live experience, not chronicle it
Small Moleskine journal, turquoise pen,
Nokia cell phone – one small concession
To husband
Texting whereabouts end of day

OK – dear back pack
With all our contents
You weighed in at just under 12 pounds
Desired ratio for my weight!!!
Adventure of a lifetime....
480 miles through French Pyrenees mountains
Across Northern Spain to Santiago de Compostelo,
Loyal backpack
My constant companion
Never causing pain
Hugging me entire way!
Forever etched in my heart
like the journey

Kathleen Plant Lov

Richard met me in Spain, and we traveled to the countryside before moving back to Nevada City, California full time from London. We stopped in New York for a few days to see the city again and rendezvous with Ben who at the time was going to Wesleyan college in Connecticut. One afternoon as we were walking through Central Park with the solid gold and red autumn leaves I became aware of a very fashionably dressed couple we had been following for a very long time. He was talking on the phone the entire time, and she was walking beside him. Something in me needed to look at her face, so I quickly walked in front of them. In that moment of looking back at her, I saw what I had been; a corporate wife, in the lonely, hollowed existence of appearances instead of heart-directed living. I felt it viscerally in my body; every cell was activated with sadness and loneliness. I had been taught duty, duty, duty my entire life. Do what you are supposed to do. Now, I wanted to follow my heart. I would sing my own version of the Christmas song, "Jingle Bells," replacing "the horse knows the way to carry the sleigh" to my version "my heart knows the way to carry me through my day. My heart does know the way!"

This visceral experience brought me back to why I was the way I was. Why duty prevailed before myself at all costs.

CHAPTER FIVE

EMOTIONALLY DEVASTATED

The summer after I turned eleven, Jane came to our home. She had platinum-blonde hair and was as beautiful as a movie star, like Marilyn Monroe. Her husband worked with my father. She pulled up into our lazy Mormon suburban neighborhood in a red convertible with the top down. She had on a light peach chiffon dress and had patent-leather shoes and belt to match, cinching her small waist. When she sat next to me, she showed me how to file my nails slowly, going one direction only. She invited me to go out with her that evening, and we would spend the night there. My dad was agitated when we left. He must have known something I didn't know. My sister wanted to go, and he started hitting her as we were walking out the door. He was in a foul mood.

At the home where the party was, a man was in the kitchen making screwdrivers. How apropos this would turn out to be. Jane gave me one. I said I was a Mormon, and I couldn't drink alcohol, and I was too young She tasted it, and said she couldn't taste alcohol, and told me to drink. I drank it. The next thing I know we are on a bed, and she is at the headboard holding me. All the men were taking turns having sex with me. As I share this story with you I realize I have no memory of what happened after that or how I felt. I was completely shut down. The wisdom of my body protected me from the effects of trauma at the time. The tears are flowing now, though, as I am connecting and releasing the emotions.

The next morning, Jane dropped me off at my house. Later on, I had scriptures from the bible I had to memorize for my church group with girls my age. I remember bringing the phone outside to the porch with its long cord just making it. It was a hot summer day and I sat on the silver Winter Dairy milk box. I called my teacher. I told her I had my three scriptures memorized, and could I recite them to her on the phone. I had never done anything like that before. It was totally out of character for the good girl I was. But something had changed in me the night before. She replied "Yes, of course." I had them bookmarked in the bible. Opening to one at a time and reading it straight from the Bible until I finished all three. I now labeled myself a bad girl. Bad girls do bad things. I didn't care and I didn't feel guilty.

Today I realize how my unrecognized rage over what happened the night before became the catalyst for cheating on my scriptures and not caring or feeling guilty. Yet, I chose to label myself a bad person. Being gang-raped and betrayed by a friend of the family left me feeling like I must have done something wrong to deserve this. Later I found out my father was entangled in this betrayal.

CHAPTER SIX

MY FATHER – THE MURDER

When I was young and living In Salt Lake City, we all loved to sleep outside on the balcony on hot summer nights. I remember one night my dad letting out a loud swear word in the middle of the night! It turned out my hamster had gotten loose and had run over his hand, arm, and chest; scaring the heck out of him. We did manage to catch the hamster and get it back into its cage.

I remember looking at my dad when I was a little girl and thinking, "I have the most handsome father ever." I thought he was just as handsome as a movie star — six feet tall, dark brown shiny hair, hazel eyes, and a grin that lit up the world. When I was in grade school I loved it when he would talk to me about the planets, gravity, and physics. I thought he was the most brilliant man ever. When friends would come over he was playful and fun. Everyone loved my father.

My father loved nice things and bought a new car every four years. He had high-end stereo equipment he would play at nearly full volume. He loved musicals and western songs. I liked to play with his albums and hold them in my small hands, looking at the images on the covers. We had a new yellow-and-white boat we used on Saturdays to waterski with our friends, and neighbors, Ruth and Boyd, and their daughters, Karen and Diane. We would pack our new blue Chevrolet station wagon with delicious picnics my mother and Ruth would prepare and always had a bag of red licorice to snack on while we were driving the hour to get to the lake and continued to eat once there. My dad and Boyd would get the boat launched, and we would play and have a fantastic time in it for the entire day. We would be in and out of the water; skiing, laughing, telling jokes, eating, and just having fun. In the winter I went snow skiing with my dad, mostly just he and I, and sometimes my uncle Bud and dear cousin, Debbie.

My father had a terrible temper. He could be laughing one moment, and in a blink of an eye he could turn into a monster – yelling, screaming, swearing, and grabbing me by my hair or anything he could get hold of, to start beating me. Usually, the offense was something trivial like spilling milk, yet at the same time I could skip school or crash the family car, and he would laugh and say, "Well, I hope you learned your lesson and won't be doing that again."

My father aspired to be a doctor, until one day, while he was working on a helicopter a wire snapped and hit his left eye blinding him. He had several operations, but his eye was never restored to normal. His doctor dream was dead and gone. Instead, he worked at Hill Air Force Base as a civilian. It was 30 miles from Salt Lake City where we lived.

My father left Hill Air Force Base to go into business with his brother, father, and another man they all knew. They formed a construction company. They put in a bid as a subcontractor with a larger company for a big job in South Dakota. They won the job. Something happened though, preventing the job from being completed. Theirs was the longest lawsuit at that time in the history of South Dakota. The judge died and they had to start over. All kinds of things happened, causing it to be so long. Finally a verdict was awarded, and it was a win for my father. Everyone was elated but that lasted only briefly. It was ruled that only the main construction company would be rewarded money, and any subcontractor would have to file a lawsuit on their own. The original lawsuit had gone on for years.

He took me with him to the company that had just been awarded the money, and he was screaming and swearing at the top of his lungs that his company needed to be paid. "Fuck the judges! It was only honest and right!" Everyone in that office froze, and you could hear a pin drop when he finished. Then two huge, strong men came and picked him up by his collar and threw him out of the building. Now he was really furious. I followed him with my head hung low in humiliation.

We got into his white pickup truck and before my door was even fully closed, he sped out of the parking lot, making the turn onto the street on two wheels. We drove for a bit on the country road. We were out of the suburbs and it was rural. There was a boy about 12 years old walking; my father stopped, rolled down his window, and offered the boy a ride home. The boy got in, but then instead of turning where he was told, my dad swerved onto an old, abandoned road and drove as far as he could over the rocks and bumps and then stopped.

He made us both get out. He said, "One of you will live and one will die. Who is it going to be?" Out of terror I screamed, "I don't want to die!" He hit the boy over the head with a huge rock, killing him, and then glared at me saying, "You did it. You chose!" Then my father raped me. He dragged the boy's body behind some big rocks and bushes.

He shoved me into the truck and was speeding when we got pulled over by a police officer. He told the police officer I had fallen and gotten hurt, and he was trying to hurry to get me home. I looked a mess, to say the least. The officer flashed his flashlight on me and around the truck. He let us go and said to drive slowly and get that girl home and taken care of. In that moment I made a decision that I was bad, which resulted in the murder of the boy. I had been the one who caused this by screaming, "I don't want to die," and I made a vow to punish myself; a vow of unhappiness. I decided that for the rest of my life I didn't deserve to be happy. So this became the undercurrent of my life; even though I would forget the vow, it would show up again and again and again throughout my life. I didn't deserve happiness. I was a bad person. (Tears are flowing down my face and my heart aches thinking and writing about this). Nothing ever came of this that I know of. I was only 10 years old at the time. The accuracy of what happened has shown up in my trauma therapy, hypnosis, as well as working with psychics and other modalities. All I know for sure is my own truth of what happened.

That summer I went to Girl Scout camp with my cousin, Debbie. One night in the middle of the night I woke up and started to cry. I was crying like I always did in my bedroom in the basement. Silent tears, until a river of tears would make my pillow damp and warm, and then I would fall back to sleep. But this time my crying turned from silent to wailing in a nano second. I was out of control. I couldn't control my racking sobs and loud crying. This wasn't like sweet and shy me, always concerned for everyone around me, the good girl, the sweet girl. I was having a full-blown nervous breakdown. Soon all the lights at camp were on and a sweet teenager, our counselor, was holding me and rocking me back and forth, saying sweet things to soothe me. She stroked my hair, singing to me, and rocking me. I don't know how long this lasted; it seemed like forever. Finally she got me calmed down and I went back to bed. No one spoke of it the next day. It was as if it didn't happen. My cousin never brought it up. Camp was over and my parents came to pick me up. When my mother saw me she whispered in my ear in a very stern voice, "I hope you didn't say anything that would embarrass our family."

I was broken into a billion shards of glass. My heart hurt, but I had to hide it from the outside world so no one would know the truth. I got good at pretending. I pretended so much it became a reality for my life. I got so good at laughing and smiling and being nice and polite, so no one had an inkling of the nightmare in which I lived. The pain was buried so deep. But sometimes when I went to bed, I would cry silently so no one could hear me. I remember once crying so hard that my entire pillowcase was wet with warm tears, and these warm tears soothed me so I could finally fall to sleep.

CHAPTER SEVEN

GROWING UP

As a baby, my mom would tell me how people always stopped her in the street and say that they had never seen such a beautiful, wide-awake baby. I didn't close my eyes because I didn't want to miss anything, even as a baby! Our family doctor told my mother he had never seen such a bright baby. He wanted to give me an intelligence test, but just prior to the test taking place my father slapped me across my face for not eating my baby cereal and I came down with a huge fever. I was only six months old. I was a good girl who always wanted to please everyone around me. I was an adorable baby, a cute young kid, but by fifth grade, I was so skinny and gawky. I had legs that looked like a giraffe and teeth as big and crooked as could be. My permanent teeth were extremely slow coming in. I had to wait until I was 15 for my molars to come in and before my orthodontist could give me braces. I couldn't speak to anyone outside of my family and close friends. If one of my teachers asked me a question, I shrugged that I didn't know even though I did know. I was terrified and too shy to talk in front of the class with everyone's eyes upon me.

I also had fun, miraculous things — like going to Yellowstone with my parents when I was just two. They looked out the cabin window and saw me frolicking with a bear cub. The mama bear saw me at the same time my parents did and charged. My dad got me out of harm's way just in the nick of time. That was one of our family stories told over and over and over again. Bears are my totem, and when I was older and lived in nature, I had so many visitations by bears. I deeply love and adore them.

We moved to a new neighborhood in Salt Lake City where houses were just being built. The neighbors who lived across the street had two girls a little older than I was, and they would babysit for our family. Throughout my younger childhood years, in the evenings all the neighborhood children would gather, and we would play "No bears are out at night" and jump rope for hours with all the fun jump-roping songs. We would sneak Jell-O out of our mothers' cupboards and eat it by licking our fingers and dipping them into the colored sugary granules. It was fun playing outside with a whole neighborhood of friends.

When I was six years old I got red snow skis for Christmas. These skis were a highlight for me as a little girl. They developed my love of sport, and to this day I continue to snow ski. I loved being outside with my dad skiing, it was a way of bonding with him. Although sometimes he would tease me and it would go too far; like telling me when the lift stopped that it was broken, and we would have to jump down and possibly break our legs or neck. This was terrifying for a small child to hear.

I was the oldest of four kids and babysitting by the time I was 10 years old earning 30 cents an hour. I was always very responsible and able as a child. If I babysat in a messy house, I would have it clean and sparkling by the time the parents returned home. By the time I was 13, I was able to save and afford to buy expensive shoes from Castleton's. For most of my life I have had a shoe fetish. Additionally, I saved to buy fabric so I could make my own clothing. I was a messy seamstress. There were always pins and fabric all over the floor that I would have to clean up.

Once I reached the fifth grade we had a chin-up contest for the entire school. I went outside to the monkey bars to see how many I could do. I couldn't even do one! Every day at recess I went out and practiced. On the day of the championship, I did more chin-ups than the boys in the sixth grade. More than everyone. I had done 20 full chin-ups. I had won the championship.

It was winter and we were sitting at the breakfast table, and my dad commented that my mom hadn't cooked the eggs properly. She said she cooked them just like she always did. But with that he backhanded her so hard she flew across the kitchen, hit her head on a wall, and fell to the floor, unconscious. I ran to her, thinking she was dead. Tears were pouring out of my eyes and falling onto her face. But then she opened her eyes. She told me, "Be a good girl, get your parka and brush your teeth." It was nearly time for my uncle Bud and Debbie to pick up my father and me to go skiing. I replied, "NO, I will not go with him after what he has done to you!" She told me, "Be a good girl and go." So, one more time, I put on my smile and my cheerful face and got into their car talking and laughing like nothing had happened.

The outside world wouldn't know the nightmare in which I lived in my own home. I hid the truth from everyone, pretending everything was fine. I put on a happy face, but I wasn't! Sometimes when we would go snow skiing my father's teasing would go too far, like telling me when the lift stopped that it was broken and that we would have to jump down, and we might break our legs or neck. And then I would feel absolutely terrified!

We lived close to a Mormon Church and I walked there on Sundays alone. My dad was atheist and my mother was Mormon. She went to church regularly from childhood but after marrying my father, he insisted she not attend. Growing up in a split-religion household was difficult for me. When I would return home from church my father would ridicule me when I shared some of the things I had learned. I enjoyed going because I was learning about God and all of my best friends were there. It made me feel like an outsider showing up alone at church, without my family.

In my eighth-grade math class, the students were required to bring in famous quotes. I remember vividly bringing in the quote: "The difficult is that which can be done immediately, the impossible is that which takes a little longer." I had to hand-paint a large banner that went above the chalk board with this quote on it. It was up for the remainder of the year. This would become the motto of how I live my life.

When I was 15 my father was transferred at work and we moved to Vienna, Virginia, where he was employed by the Pentagon, and would later help me get a summer job there. Across the street was a European family, and once again I was babysitting in the neighborhood.

The neighbors had a library of books which were amazing and I found erotic books that I had never seen in my life, and I liked reading them. As I read I was thinking of the first boy I had ever kissed.

Each summer my family and cousins from Winchester, Virginia would stay in rented houses next to each other at Virginia Beach. I met Jim, a handsome boy next door, who had a red convertible and was staying with his parents. He asked me out on a date to go to a movie. I was sixteen and very excited. My father said NO boys. Boys only wanted one thing from girls and that was sex. I was furious with my father for not letting me go to a movie with a nice boy who was with his parents. I ended up going over to Jim's house one day when my family and his parents had gone to the beach. We had the house to ourselves. I drank my first beer. It made me dizzy. He kissed me. It was my first kiss.

He asked me why I was so nervous around him. I said, "I don't know, I just feel scared and nervous around boys." He said, "You are so beautiful, you need to let go of that old feeling and belief." Then he gave me his favorite stone that was very smooth and fit right into my hand. He told me if I ever felt scared or nervous just to hold the stone and it would soothe me and that it was filled with his good thoughts and feelings toward me. I wonder what happened to that stone.

In retrospect, I realize I was an emotionally innocent 16-year-old who had her first kiss and first beer, against the backdrop of being gang-raped and also sexually molested by my father. No wonder I was nervous.

A recurring nightmare I had for so many years of my life: I am in the basement of my grandparents' home playing with a friend. Two men come in and are trying to kill me. There is a little window up high, and if I stand on my friend's shoulders I can reach the window and escape. I am on the street, when suddenly there are headlights. The men are hunting me down. I jump behind bushes to hide. My heart is pounding. I wake up in a sweat.

Many years later I learned how to have lucid dreams. I could look for something in a dream that would let you know you were dreaming. Once I realized I was in a dream, I could work with the dream. When I was in my late twenties, I tried this. Realizing I was in my recurring nightmare, I turned to the men and asked them who they were and what they were doing. The reply came, "We are fear, and we have come from your dad. He wanted you to be a good girl." After we had that exchange, the nightmare stopped. I never had it again.

Every year from the time I was 12 I would miss at least a week of school due to strep throat. When I was 17 I discovered the book, *Psycho Cybernetics*, a book about human self-image; how it is crafted and how it can drastically change your happiness and success and life.

From reading that book I learned that I could interrupt an illness as soon as I would become aware of it taking hold in my body. I would start to say to myself, "The point of power is in the present moment, and I choose to feel and be healthy and well." I would repeat this over and over like a silent mantra and visualize myself being healthy and well. What I saw in my mind's eye was a healthy body and mind. I knew this to be true for myself, and also what would occur. I stopped getting strep throat from then on. I used this technique to raise my self-confidence, too. That book had an amazing effect on my life.

We never stop learning. There are layers and layers of learning process throughout life. In writing this part of my journey I was curious about what was the deeper emotional significance of a strep throat. So, I consulted Louise Hay's book, *Heal Your Body*, where she writes about these connections. I found out: Strep Throat is Swallowed Anger. Being Stifled. And a Sore Throat is: Holding in angry words and feeling unable to express the self.

This was a big a-ha for me. My strep throat had me in bed listless from the unspoken deep burning rage in my throat.

Our bodies respond to our feelings and emotional traumas. Illness becomes manifest because of this. Each individual illness will reflect an emotion. My understanding of these concepts and applying them to my life created significant positive changes. I embraced that I had the power to change and create my reality. This is when I let my hair grow long and began to appreciate my beautiful figure. I was no longer skinny and gawky, my braces were off, and I had beautiful teeth. A new life was opening to me.

I had been invited to sit in the cafeteria during lunch with the popular kids. We all had fake IDs, and we would go to Georgetown University "Campus Club" to dance. Alcohol was served there so you had to be eighteen. I got asked to dance by my friend's cousin who was 23. We slowly danced to *Something* by the Beatles, and he broke off a six-year relationship to be with me.

We dated my whole senior year. I loved him, but I wasn't ready to settle down. I had plans to go to college in Utah. After a long time of only making out and shortly before going to college, we actually had sexual intercourse. Afterward, I started crying hysterically. I jumped into my dad's car to go home. I smashed the car into the garage door. I was hysterical and I couldn't stop crying and didn't know why. Of course now, I know exactly why. Being penetrated by someone I loved triggered the sexual molestation from my early years by my father — and the gang-rape.

My love/hate relationship with my father showed itself again and again. When I left for college he was the one who took me shopping for suitcases and a trunk. He flew me out to Utah and got me set up. I remember feeling so excited and walking toward my dorm after saying good-bye to my dad. For some reason, I turned around and caught a glance of such a sad expression on his face, hauntingly sad. Little did I know at that time all of the traumas I would uncover about our relationship.

While in college I would go home to Virginia for the summers, where I worked for clothing and spending money. My father got me a secretarial job at the Pentagon.

While I was in Virginia I traveled to my first yoga class in Washington, DC. I am directionally dyslexic and always going the wrong direction and getting lost. But after my first yoga class that summer it felt like I just put my feet up on the dashboard and the car drove itself home with ease and grace and flow. I had never experienced anything like it!

I graduated from college with a degree in textiles/business and found that the pay in Utah was not adequate. There was not much of a fashion industry there. I realized I could get a job as a cocktail waitress working three evenings a week and skiing during the day. I decided to return to school because I could see that I had a deep love for children, and I wanted to teach. I received my second degree in Early Childhood Education, but that career path didn't pan out as I had planned. One evening working at the Hilton hotel, I realized that I wanted to follow my heart and use my textiles/business degree. I was looking at the green emergency exit sign at work which seemed to be pulsating, screaming to me, "It's time to 'EXIT' to leave, it's time to get a career." It was time, and I decided to move to California. I was 27 and I knew that cocktailing wasn't going to take me anywhere; it was time for a proper career using my textiles and business degree.

One night four women drinking in my section had asked me if a man sitting at the booth next to them was Barry Gibb of the BeeGee's. I asked him, and it wasn't. He was sitting alone and laughed when I asked him, and then he asked for my number, and I said, "No, I don't give out my number to customers," but he got my number by the end of that evening. His name is Bill. We casually dated for a couple of months even though I told him I was going to move to Los Angeles. We had a great time together, a lot of fun. He offered to drive with me in my car with the small amount of belongings I was taking into my new life in California. The upscale hotel chain where I cocktailed had given me enough vouchers to make it to Los Angeles, staying in a hotel room each night on the way there. We took our time driving and having fun. He was traveling with me so that he could pick up a car to drive back to Salt Lake City. He loved Porsches, and he was brokering a Carrera in Salt Lake City, so it was going to be a fun trip back for him. At some point he noticed that I was directionally dyslexic, always going the wrong way, and when we got to the city he helped me navigate, bought me a map, and told me that the ocean faces west. After he left, I found a couple temporary places to live and had a few detours of working as a cocktail server in Santa Monica and on Rodeo Drive in Beverly Hills. I then had some modeling jobs and was later hired by Saks Fifth Avenue to be a buyer. A new friend told me that being a sales representative was far more fun. Soon, I found what would become a great job and went to work for Levi Strauss, starting at the bottom counting Levi jeans in department stores. I went through several months of hell watching other people being promoted over me. I wasn't the right body type or demeanor for a woman they thought could be successful.

One of their sales reps who had been a star professional football player got fired for totally neglecting all his clients. It was a hornet's nest. I was asked to take care of his territory until they could find a replacement. Funny thing, I loved my clients. I would look at their stores as if they were mine and I would produce plans and strategies that would bring them success. They loved working with me and they trusted me. I was rookie of the year. The following year when I had my own territory, I was sales representative of the year at Levi Strauss Los Angeles.

One of the adventures I stumbled upon in California was a new-age church that had different events and speakers. One night it was someone who was leading a past-life regression. Each of us there was led by her words to go deeper into a hypnotic state, taking us to a significant past life we had experienced. We were guided to take notice of our shoes, and mine were Native American beaded moccasins. My vision was of my father as an Indian chief who died because I rocked the canoe and it got caught in bushes and he drowned. He was the father who loved me with all his heart and soul, who was so kind and loving and wise. I was at fault for his death, I blamed myself and was unhappy in that life after this happened. That night my heart ached so badly I could not stop crying. When I went to leave this event, I had to sit in my car for well over an hour to compose myself enough to drive. My experience was emotionally devastating. I had actually been there in a different time, experiencing my father's death with this accident being my fault. I had an understanding of someone loving me so deeply and feeling profound loss. This vision was such a contrast to how my father was in this life, compared to the Native American chief. Even today I can feel the sadness of this contrast.

When I was 30 I had a sales meeting in Las Vegas. I was talking to my father on the phone. He said he had some work in Las Vegas and would be there as well and we could go out to a show that evening. He got a room for us, and I arrived at the theater just in time for the show. They served alcoholic drinks, and I had a margarita. Then we went upstairs to our room. I walked in and it was very late, and I was extremely tired, ready to jump into my pajamas and into my bed. I saw only one bed, and I told my father I was going to call the front desk and get another room. I was just about to make the call when he said it was the last room and all they had was one bed. I went into the bathroom and put on my pajamas. I went to my side of the bed and as I was getting in, I looked up as my dad was just removing his boxers and lifting the covers to get in with me, naked. I was upset and freaked out. I couldn't believe he would consider this to be appropriate behavior with me. I spent that night half awake, clinging to my side. Looking back on this moment I can vividly remember how absolutely disgusted I felt by his actions toward me.

CHAPTER EIGHT

MY MOTHER

My mother, Bonnie Lee Stewart Plant, was so beautiful! Looking at her when I was a little girl, I told her she had beautiful legs. She did! And she was beautiful from her head to the tips of her toes. I remember when I was in the seventh grade, French twists were very popular for women in my mom's generation. She would go to the beauty parlor every week to have it done.

She was good with money and so was my dad. They kept track of their money and mom stretched her food allowance with coupons and an S & H Green Stamps Book. You would fill it in and then redeem it for something you wanted depending on the points you had accumulated.

My parents both worked hard. Mom had four children by the time I was ten, three girls and a boy. She was a fabulous cook. On Sundays I loved roast beef, mashed potatoes and gravy, green beans or in the summer, fresh corn from the farm stand a block away, along with sliced cucumbers in vinegar and warm juicy tomatoes sliced with salt and pepper. I liked to drink the vinegar from the cucumber bowl as I was clearing the table. We always had dessert on Sundays; peach cobbler with whipped cream poured over it hot out of the oven, or strawberries and cream, ice cream or watermelon in the summer.

Mom kept the house looking beautiful and clean. Having an alcoholic father who lived in the bar was a great embarrassment to my mother. This was her deep wound. Being poor as a child was an amount of shame for my mother as was feeling different, less than, hungry, getting nothing for Christmas, and only a few times receiving an apple for a present. She had promised herself she was not going to be poor again. The price of that vow was a husband who could turn into a monster on a dime and go into a rage and hurt someone. So not wanting ever to be poor again created a cage around her. She would never leave my father. That was it. We never knew which one of us he would come after. It was always a game of roulette as I sat watching and waiting and praying it wouldn't be me this time, but it often was. I am a truth sayer, and I wouldn't back down from what I felt was true. Even beatings couldn't get me to back down. My mother asked me once if I could please just be like the other children and keep my mouth shut. But I couldn't. Later in life she acknowledged me and thanked me for my courage.

I always had mom's message that things were more important than feelings or people. Don't get me wrong, she was such a loving, kind person; always checking in on her friends and was there with a Popsicle for the neighborhood kids. She took care of us with the awesome food she made. It was so amazing to come home from school and smell a whiff of the cinnamon rolls baking and then eating them hot out of the oven with butter on top.

THE QUEEN BEE

Imagine curvy lush tree lined streets
Vibrant colors and sensuous warm breezes
Then God taking a huge cosmic straw sucking out all juiciness
Leaving instead straight and narrow streets on a grid

Straight and narrow people live on the straight and narrow streets,
In bland brick houses with cement porches
They are the "chosen people," others are to be converted or tolerated
Fear of hell and church three times a week keep them righteous and good

Here to propagate the Earth, they marry young and breed fast
Through hot desert summers and harsh winters
With the strength of the surrounding mountains
They refrain, restrain, and abstain from coffee tea or alcohol

As a child my family ate Jell-o in 50 different styles
I ate Fruit Loops smothered with white sugar
In summer we had fresh tomatoes and corn eaten in cool canyons
At night we played Kick the Can, Hide and Seek and No Bears are Out

My mother had all the necessary skills
Mending and sewing and cooking big meals served with milk
The house would have smelled like Lysol
Except my father's cigarette smoke smothered all else

KATHLEEN PLANT LOV

*Everything comes to a standstill on the day of the Sabbath
Little League games and holidays get moved to other days of the week
In cities or quaint towns with names like Nephi and Moroni.
organ music belts out the hymns*

*The individual gives way to the group, the group
to the head of the church
This male head of the church decrees how to live; even how to vote
For a State whose symbol is the beehive.*

*This doesn't really make Sense
Everyone knows the hive is run by the Queen, not the drone!*

Kathleen Plant Lov

When I was young we played games at night before going to bed — Uncle Wiggly or Old Maid and other games as well. I hated to get the old maid card and would stick it slightly higher in my hand and was surprised how my mom always fell for my trick by picking that card!

Even when my dad would have one of his explosions and one of us would get hurt, she never even considered leaving him. Having a nice home, a nice station wagon, nice children, with nice clothes, was more important to her than anything.

The price was that she went unconscious to do this. I remember watching her working so hard – scrubbing floors on her hands and knees and never complaining. She always felt so vacant to me. She wasn't fully present. Part of her lived inside herself only.

Now I can see how I repeated my mother's pattern of becoming unconscious to make my marriage work.

My mom was proud of me because I was a hard worker, babysitting since I was ten years old and taking care of my younger siblings including my youngest brother who was born 10 years after I was. Not only did I care for my siblings, I also babysat the children in the neighborhood.

Once, my mom made felt skirts for my sister who was two years younger than I, and one for myself. My sister's was blue and mine was red, and they had fish of another color sewn on with bubbles. They were so adorable. My mom could be very creative at times. I remember looking at her and studying her and she didn't look joyous or happy. She often looked like she was in a trance performing all the duties of a mother and housewife. I don't remember her just giggling or ever laughing really hard. She was good at sports, slalom waterskiing, and really good at bowling, and so was my dad. They played on teams weekly with their friends, and they played bridge on the weekends. They enjoyed people and we all had fun with our water-skiing boat by inviting friends and having big picnics and fantastic food to eat, but away from her friends my mom often seemed preoccupied and distant. Beyond an exact memory, just a feeling.

Looking back, I now understand how my mom put money and security first. She stayed with my dad because he could provide for the family nicely. That was the priority. Her security and things were more important than her heart and body, as well as ours. Money, appearances, security, and what the neighbors thought of us ran my mother's world and way of doing things. I know it wasn't just my mom, it was America, it was the fifties. It was more than a family thing, it was cultural. Things were placed higher than people. To divorce would take my mom back to the trauma of her parents being divorced, the stigma of divorce. And what, for heaven's sake, would the neighbors think! Tears well up as I really feel this for the first time. Her staying with my father kept all of us in harm's way. I have come to understand that I had a deep wound because of this, money and things taking priority. I remember begging my mother to leave my father. I told her we could make it without him. I pleaded with her, but she wouldn't even engage in the conversation. (Now I am crying.)

I've often wondered why my mother didn't protect me from my father's constant sexual molestation of me.

When I was eleven my father built me my own bedroom in the basement. I was so excited to have my own room. My sister, who was two years younger, and I fought too much and my parents wanted to separate us. It was a beautiful room, it even had an entry way to my walk-in closet with a lovely ivory-colored vanity with a mirror at one end. I felt so special having my very own gorgeous bedroom. I remember choosing my bedspread; it looked like satin but was probably rayon and the colors were greens, blues and purples. After sharing a room with my sister for so many years I felt blessed to have my own room away from everyone. It was a sanctuary that I loved. I wrote in my journal, read my books, and enjoyed my beloved stuffed animals on my bed. It was a special place to hang out with my girlfriends without anyone annoying us. I was so thankful to my father for this magical space. This gratitude and excitement was short-lived as my sanctuary, though, and very quickly, became my torture chamber. One night, while I was sleep, my father came into my room. I was awakened when he climbed into my bed naked. I felt disgust and fear as he began to touch me, kiss me, and sexually penetrate me. There I was, down stairs all alone. My sanctuary had become a dungeon in hell. The polarity of love and hate was being shattered because all I felt in the moment was hate.

My father coming down every night was my fear. I waited in the dark, scared. Such mixed feelings. Feelings of love and hate. I thought my father was the smartest man in the whole world, and the most handsome and clever. He could fix anything and talked to me about physics. Yet each night he came downstairs and stole from my soul, from my young body, which was not his to take. I loved and hated the same person. He could love me and inflict pain, could beat me, and molest me. All these secrets lived inside of me at such an early age. No wonder I lost my voice. I could only speak at home and with my friends. I couldn't speak at school. I couldn't stand eyes looking at me. I would mumble "I don't know," even though I really did, just to keep from having to speak and use my voice. I didn't share my thoughts and my words for fear of people looking at me. I now know through my trauma therapy, there were sexual things that went on with other people looking at me and doing bad things to me. It wasn't just my dad. My mother once told me my father had such a huge sexual drive that he had to have sex with her every single night or he would become mean and nasty. Part of this routine was that he would then get up and go smoke a cigarette. He would come have sex with me after he completed with her. I don't remember much about this. I slept with my back on the wall so that I could hear and see when my door opened.

I also remember the innocence about the pain of making a mistake of any kind, tiny or large, in my life. My conception was a mistake. My mother told me that my father shoved her into their car and took her on a bumpy road trying to force a miscarriage. But my spirit was resolute that I would come to earth at that time and I was born and everyone loved me.

When I was four years old I left my doll's baby buggy, which I had been given for Christmas, outside in the rain and it got ruined. My dad started hitting me and screaming at me for what I had done. But I hadn't known rain could ruin something. I turned into a perfectionist in many areas of my life because I was so frightened I might make a mistake and be punished and hurt for it. I lived in a strait jacket of fear. This fear played out other times in my life, and I did get hurt. Many years later I learned to break that thought pattern by using my five senses to create a different reality.

My dad's ongoing abuses over the years in addition to pounding my mom's head into the concrete porch and his affair with a much younger secretary who he later married, were catalysts for mom's divorce. After their divorce, my mom was happier than I had ever seen her before. My mother was amazing in the way she worked, managed her home, and fixed up the downstairs, turning it into an apartment for income. She went back to work for Deloitte and Touche, a large financial services company. Her house was always cared for inside and outside with help of the boys she hired to weed and mow the lawn.

Mom loved to decorate and every so often her house would get a major remodel to bring it up to date. She liked pretty things, and we have that in common.

The vacant stare my mom had left her after she divorced my father. She actually thrived. She had tons of friends in the Mormon church. Even though she didn't believe in the church, she was a social member. Oh my God, she loved basketball. You could hear her whooping and hollering while watching a basketball game. She worked in downtown Salt Lake City with her friend and neighbor, Karen. They would get season passes to watch the Jazz play basketball, and boy could my mom ever cheer. She hadn't been a cheerleader for nothing!

My mom was psychic through her dreams, even though she never developed it. Her mom was psychic, too, and could read coffee grounds. I think it must be something that has been passed down on her side of the family because I too have vivid dreams sometimes that inform my inner and outer life. Now I am learning to stop and really listen to them.

Mom had visitation dreams throughout her life. She also had vivid dreams she would remember, and she would share them with me. I remember one time being in her home visiting with her and she had a dream that her departed sister and two brothers came to her and said, "Bonnie, come. We are waiting for you in heaven." She told them, "No! I'm not ready yet!"

Mom wasn't ready to transition yet, which led me to wonder if I am ready to change the conditions of life moving forward with Richard. Reflecting on my childhood has enlightened me. My childhood was filled with abuse and fear. I see how this permeates my marriage. Richard didn't beat me, it was a different type of abuse. I really didn't matter to him, just like I didn't really matter to my dad in a healthy way. My mom ignored my abuse and turned the other way. I remember my mom also ignoring me coming home and telling her about the doctors that had molested me. They are too numerous to mention them all. I was taught to trust our doctors; that they had our best interest at heart. Maybe one day years ago they did.

When I was around 15, I got braces! My orthodontist would line all of his tools on my chest and then fumble around finding the right tool he needed while touching my breasts instead of using the table to put his tools on. When I would come home upset and tell my mother what had happened she would reply with, "You are so flat-chested, and you have a wild imagination!" It felt so creepy, and I had to keep going and enduring this because my mother didn't believe a doctor or orthodontist could be capable of such a thing. It was horrible having it happen and was made worse because my mother, my own parent, couldn't hear me and protect me inside my home or out.

In high school, I had a radiant, clear, beautiful complexion, but one day I had a pimple, and I was so freaked out, I missed school. I had my mom get me an appointment with our family doctor. I was 17. I went to the doctor and he held my face up to the light to look at it better with his hand on my chin and maneuvering my face. He said, "What a beautiful face!" and kissed me on my mouth. I jumped off the table and ran out of his office into the car. By now it was no use telling my mother. She didn't believe these things happened to me.

Just like my mother ignored my complaints and needs around doctors' abuse and disrespect, I have been ignoring Richard's abuse and disrespect and turning the other way like I have done for so many years with my family and doctors. Unfortunately at this point in my life, I still carried the belief that if I tried hard enough, gave my all, then things would change. And I had my highest hopes that Richard and I would rekindle our love in Nevada City after he left the corporate world.

CHAPTER NINE

NEVADA CITY

Richard left the corporate world, I never knew why. We had purchased a 28-acre property complete with an architecturally designed house, a swimming pool, beautiful entryway covered with gorgeous clematis flowers, freestanding office, and guest cottage. It was within walking distance of a lake where you could only kayak, no motorboats allowed. There was another larger lake right next to it where we could waterski. The boys could wakeboard when Ben and his friends visited. I was in love with the woods, and that is where I wanted to spend all my time. I taught exercises from the book *The Artist's Way* to a group of friends in Mill Valley. I would drive there once a month to do this. Now I was fully living a life that had heart and meaning to me.

Richard had been asked to teach a class on leadership at UC Davis graduate school, which was just an hour away. One day he told me all the kids in the class wanted me to come and speak to them about what it was like to be the wife of the president of a huge company. He told me, "Just tell them the truth." They asked me questions and I answered honestly. If you do not keep putting wood on the fire, it dies out, and it's the same with relationships. I told them how Richard made his work his priority and the effect it had on me, and our marriage. It was really hard, and I was not happy coming in last all the time and not being a priority in his life. I cannot remember the whole class, but women and men had tears in their eyes, and a few were crying. The Dean told Richard that my time with them had been profound, and how deeply touched they were. UC Davis was a wonderful experience. To be real and do what I love is my commitment - to always come from my heart. I only want love, light, and truth in my life.

IT WAS AT THIS POINT THAT I PROFOUNDLY BEGAN TO CHANGE MY LIFE.

I attended a Robert Haas Poetry Workshop in Grass Valley. I had a tremendous thirst for poetry. Robert was a former poet laureate of the United States. I bought one of his books and asked him to autograph it for me. He wrote, "In every class I teach there is always one person who holds the bar of truth for everyone else. You were that person today. Thank you!"

This is the poem I wrote at his workshop.....

THE AUTUMN WIND BITES

What am I avoiding?
A dream journal next to my nightstand
Images flow in the morning.
Will I use what I am given

KATHLEEN PLANT LOV

People say dreams are fleeting
But isn't life
Same patterns over and over
How do we forget so easily?

The autumn wind bites
The gate is still broken
What is still broken in myself?
What cold wind is biting my heart?

The trees drop their leaves
Why can't I drop what is no longer
What am I holding on to?
Fear looms in the darkness.

Kathleen Plant Lov

CHAPTER TEN

DIVORCING RICHARD

When I walked the Camino de Santiago I set an intention to walk away from my old life and emerge into a life of vibrance and empowerment with devotion to my truest self; truly a new experience was set in motion from that moment forward. It was a choice-point and I had chosen. I didn't know how that would look or unfold but I had drawn the proverbial line-in-the-sand. From that point forward without compromise or apology I was committed to living in honor of my truest and highest self. As a result, the aspects of me as a healer and mystic burst forth as if exploding; they were suppressed for so long. I could no longer not be who I really was. I had to be all of myself. I proclaimed, "This is my God-Goddess given birthright and Divine Heritage. I embrace and accept it into my new heart now."

Part of that intention was that I was done with the corporate world and being a corporate wife. I told Richard I would be moving back to California. I was shocked when he left his company and followed me. I knew it wasn't love for me that propelled that decision for him. There had to be other things going on at work that he kept to himself.

When Richard and I moved back to California we joined a golf club. The friends we made there were not really my tribe. It was okay, but my true desire was to learn to communicate with nature and explore my many interests and intuitive gifts. I studied Cellular Memory Release, a technique to go deep into the pain or trauma and keep intensifying it. At some point there is nearly always a release that takes place. I was trained to be a facilitator. I discovered I had gifts for channeling and I started to channel Mother Mary. Sadly, I was not allowed to talk about these things to Richard. He approved of me studying herbs but not channeling. I had to keep this to myself so as to not upset him because he would have angry outbursts.

I did a creative-writing course and wrote a story about a woman on a bicycle trip to France who for the first time in her life followed her passions; this character had an affair on that trip. I also wrote about the character's husband who had many affairs over the years but had been "discreet." When I finished writing, hot tears were streaming down my face. I knew in that moment my marriage was over. The truth of this had been percolating. I grabbed my jacket and ran outside. Whenever I had tears or goosebumps, I knew they were a confirmation of my truth. I knew without a doubt my marriage to Richard was complete.

One weekend while hosting the women in my year-long course on the Artist's Way we were taking turns lip syncing. I chose to lip sync the song "The Crying Game." As soon as I heard the first two lines of the song; "I know all there is to know about the crying game; I have had my share of the Crying Game," my whole body began to tremble and I fell to the floor. My friends encircled me and held me. Their love gave me the courage to finish the song.

My tears and trembling were my body's confirmation of how necessary it was to leave Richard. In my marriage of 22 years to him, I hid. My core essence as a healer, mystic, and later channeling Mother Mary was an embarrassment to Richard. For many years he wouldn't allow me to fully express myself except to my very inner circle of girlfriends. He wanted my truest gifts concealed; shackled; restrained. Just like the character in the Crying Game, I had been locked in a closet with my most authentic self-obscured by his societal expectations.

What I most wanted in our marriage was to be loved and seen and feel wanted by Richard; for him to make our relationship a priority and nurture it. Now what I wanted more than anything — more than being loved by another — was to fully be myself; all of myself; to live all the parts that had previously not been given permission to surface. I could no longer hide these precious parts of myself.

NORMAL

I've never been normal
Born with a gift of 'seeing'
Into a family whose religion was denial
This was very dangerous

When what you see is black
But you are told it is white
You stop trusting that inner voice
The voice of intuition you were born with

KATHLEEN PLANT LOV

My husband thinks channeling is weird
But loves that I am kind and nice
I love that I am weird
Anyone can act kind and nice

But I cling to the kind and nice version of myself
It is the substance that has brought me synthetic love
But now I want to taste real love
I want to taste who I really am.

D*I*V*O*R*C*E = FREEDOM TO BE

Kathleen Plant Lov

On a quiet evening at the end of November 2005, I opened my heart fully and authentically shared my feelings around the completion of our marriage with Richard. He asked, "What is the bottom line?" "Divorce," I replied. "How can you do this to our son?" he asked. I told him, "If I stay married to you I am living a lie and I feel the greatest gift I could give Ben is the gift of truth."

Richard said, "You have all the freedom in the world in our marriage. I allow you to do whatever you want." That said it all. "Allow." He told me we shouldn't waste money on expensive lawyers. He wrote on a piece of paper how much money we had and said we would split it 50-50. I had no idea of the amount of money we had, as he had it all in another bank account. I signed tax papers as he was rushing out the door.

We had always wanted to go to Oaxaca, Mexico together. Richard suggested we take one last trip and go there to say good-bye to each other and leave on a high note.

Reflecting on our marriage, I saw how I walked away from a successful career at Levi Strauss, which I loved. A-ha, it was there that I abandoned myself again. I saw a pattern of how I have abandoned myself over and over again throughout my life.

I held the belief that if I could only be loving enough, kind enough, good enough, nice enough, or work hard enough, then Richard could love me.

The housecleaners had come right after Richard moved out and I discovered that they had broken a porcelain heart from Paris that was one of the first gifts Richard had given me 22 years earlier. That felt very symbolic to me.

This reminded me of the day when I was doing a shamanic drumming journey all those years earlier with Angeles Arrien. I saw the letters D-I-V-O-R-C-E spelled in the clouds. It had been so prominent at the time but I had totally forgotten about it until now. Here it was all these years later. I was finally getting my divorce.

Clearly it was time for me to take full responsibility for the care of my soul, my self-worth, self-dignity, and self-love. There were no more excuses and no barriers to becoming.

Several months later when I was in Maui for a week-long Soul Motion dance workshop, I received the news my divorce was final. That morning, I put on the song White Bird and began to dance, immersing myself fully in the story contained in the lyrics. The song had haunted me since the first time I heard it in college in the early '70s but I never understood why... Until now.

Now I realized I had opened the door of my gilded cage. I had finally leapt and in doing so I found my wings and my freedom.

One night, as I was coming home in the dark of the evening, I found a woman standing by my front door. She wanted to ask me questions; from those questions it was clear Richard was getting vetted for a new job. He had earlier told me he wanted his work more than he wanted me. I knew how important this was to him. I answered several questions and then she asked me if he had ever hit me. I said, "No." She asked if he had ever shoved me and I said, "No." Being a truth-teller and always committed to telling the truth in my life, even when it meant a beating from my father, the part of me that wanted to protect Richard, to be a good girl and help him get this job, abandoned me and my truth. Tears are flooding down my cheeks as I write this. I replied, "No," and she had me sign papers. No matter how much work we have done, no matter how many wise words we have and our good intentions, our wounded parts can still take over. The family imprints are deep and I have spent my life learning how to listen to my heart and soul and not continue living from my wounds.

CHAPTER ELEVEN

MY FREEDOM

BARS OF GOLD

Six story house: Belgravia, London.
Five star hotels, chic restaurants,
flying first class,
Pebble Beach, British Open,
Wimbledon, Ascot.
She entertained
Latest edition of Zagat Guide-
her bible

Dining with Presidents of companies,
Senators even President Clinton,
years ago, meeting Princess Diana

Goose laying golden eggs
Secretary, personal assistant,
Executive assistant, accountant,
lawyer, silver Jaguar with driver

KATHLEEN PLANT LOV

Their job – make his easier
Hers – make his more successful
He's constantly gone
Blackberry attached to him
like invisible umbilical cord

Her hands and feet ice cold
Severe backaches, headaches
aching thirsty heart
never complaining
always smiling
$150 an hour to therapist-
Paying someone to listen
Wondering….
"What form of prostitution is this?"

Chauffeur, maid, personal trainer,
Private pilates instructor, personal shopper,
chiropractor, acupuncturist, healer
keeping her taped together
Appearing whole
Shattered is the reality

Someone said Sleeping Beauty wakes at 50
She was 50
She walked 480 miles alone across Spain
Walked away from her old life
She moved to the woods

*Closest neighbors and friends —
trees, a lake, birds, deer, bear,
coyote, snakes, lizards, frogs*

*Opening closet full of
Prada dresses, Chanel suits,
Jimmy Choo shoes
Ghosts from a past life
Very bad dream*

*She has warm hands
happy heart
wears jeans
Gives herself permission to write
Even bad poetry is better than none*

This bird is now free

— Kathleen Plant Lov

Shortly after Richard moved out around the end of 2005, I was contemplating selling the property, it was simply too big for me, but standing on my deck looking out over the beauty, the land asked me to stay ... "This land is sacred and needs to be shared with others."

Right around that same time I started to do 5 Rhythms dancing. The founder, Gabrielle Roth, designed to put the body in motion in order to still the mind. The five rhythms follow the order of Flowing, Staccato, Chaos, Lyrical, and Stillness. When danced in this sequence it is known as a "wave" and takes about an hour to dance. A dance set consisted of two waves and would finish in two hours. It had been years since I had the opportunity to do anything around my creativity and movement; I was completely shut down after my marriage. I was so shy in the first class that I went to the back of the large hall we used and stood there barely moving. It was in this class that I met Michael, the 5 Rhythms leader. After my first class many of us went out for lunch, and someone mentioned what would become MoonBear sanctuary to him. He wanted to come over to my property to see about having gatherings there. When Michael came to visit, we had a huge attraction between us. I wanted so badly to kiss him, but I didn't. He had been married three times before we got together, which gave me pause but I couldn't deny the attraction and my marriage with Richard had been non-physical for years.

Michael loved the property and we would hold monthly gatherings for the 5 Rhythms group, with a potluck, swim party, badminton, and bocce ball after. It was a lot of fun, and we really got to know each other well, which created an amazing community. He also had a radio show where he would interview famous people who were making a difference in the world. He asked me if I wanted to co-host his show, but I found out very quickly that he wanted to be in control and wanted my voice to chime in only occasionally. So, after a while, that wasn't a fit, but I certainly met some incredible people doing his show. We continued dating on and off for three years or so. He was also very romantic, loved to cook, and would be putting together his 5 Rhythms music set when we would meet for dinner at his place. He loved to pamper me and take care of me, but this came with the cost of losing myself again in a relationship.

It was incredible to be in a relationship where I was seen and valued for just who I was. To be truly loved and to have fun! I loved pulling up to his home and as I got out of my car I could hear the music pouring out of his home. We would be so happy to see each other and he would greet me with a huge hug and kiss and take me in his arms and start dancing with me.

We both wanted to expand our horizons and went to Mexico for Transformational Breathwork with founder Judith Kravitz. After that we went to the Galapagos Islands. We flew to Ecuador to the rainforest with the Achuar Indigenous people and also to Maui for a 5 Rhythms dance workshop for a week. It was actually in Maui when I got the news my divorce was final and I put on the song White Bird and started dancing. Michael looked at me with surprise and asked aren't you at all sad. I replied "no, I am only happy".

Michael and I also shared similar core wounds from our childhood but we were both ready, willing and able to work through whatever came up. It felt amazing to be loved so deeply and to have a beloved who could receive my love. We were in a romantic partner relationship for around 3 years.

I had a sweat lodge built with wooden branches making an igloo-like frame. It was covered with blankets. A fire was built by an Indigenous Native American shaman who prayed while sacred feathers fanned the fire. We were praying for the new use of the land now named MoonBear Sanctuary. We set intentions and prayed for the land to be blessed and protected. We gave prayers of gratitude to all the directions and many more prayers came forth by those attending.

Shortly thereafter I went to a meeting called "Gather The Women," just forming. I volunteered to lead monthly rituals. Other women offered to lead such things as knitting, hiking, and other group activities. I had a custom 30-foot yurt built for facilitators and myself to hold workshops and ceremonies. It had a wide wooden deck and railing surrounding it; inside the floors were hardwood. The yurt had a nice-sized wood burning stove outfitted to heat well in the winter months. Thirty feet directly across the yurt was the enchanted fairy cottage built with a pitched roofline, a deck out front, beautiful railings, and a mural inside with a background of mauve and deep red-purple madrone trees painted by artist and dear friend, Jeanine Christman. I came up with the name of MoonBear Sanctuary, because I love the moon and bears are one of my totems that have shown up throughout my life.

The monthly rituals I held at MoonBear Sanctuary were very well attended. The founder of "Gather The Women" told me it was the biggest money-maker of all the groups throughout all of the years I was there. Each woman would pay $10 to attend a group event which then went to fund GTW. Nine women showed up for my first ritual and we sat outside on my stone patio surrounded by flowers in the raised rock gardens. I first guided them in a meditation to look at what their biggest dream was then we each made dream catchers which we infused with our unique dream. I had never made one, so before we all met, I looked up how to assemble dream catchers. I had lots of thin branches from the land that could be bent into a circle, and I had items to embellish them. I also bought some wire to weave the inside together. There were fun things like beautiful small stones, beads and feathers that could be threaded into each dream catcher.

I was introduced to a woman who was an authority on creating labyrinths and was part of the labyrinth creation at Grace Cathedral in San Francisco. She told me a sign that the Divine had received the labyrinth was that water would appear over the places where a labyrinth had been built. I thought, well that won't happen here in Nevada City with our hot summers and bright blue skies and never any rain until autumn. A chalk outline of the entire labyrinth had been made in advance. All we needed to do was place the smooth river rocks that had been delivered the day before onto the chalk outline. First, I led the group of women in prayers, blessing the land and our ancestors, and blessing the stones. We prayed for creating a world of love that works for all life; for all the people who were making this labyrinth now, for all who would walk this labyrinth and in deep gratitude for all the love and prayers that would take place within this labyrinth. We would each lay a stone on the chalk outline with prayer until it was complete. Just as we finished, we looked up at the bright blue sky; little wispy lines of white clouds formed over the labyrinth making the shape of a heart. It rained ever so lightly over our new creation. Then poof! The clouds disappeared. The labyrinth and each of us had just been blessed!

I loved living in Nevada City. I had listened to the land asking me to stay after Richard had moved out. I didn't have a plan. Everything divinely unfolded. Everything was revealed and put into place to orchestrate miracles time and again.

The water well on my land was running dry. It had gone from 6 GPM (Gallons per Minute) when we purchased the property to 1 GPM! I had hired a company to drill a new well. The day they arrived to look for a new place to drill, I got out my divining rods and found a spot. The company wanted to drill in a different place, but I insisted that we use the spot I had found. My chosen location had 26 GPM when 6 GPM was the average for the area. I love that I was now trusting my guidance and not that of the "authorities!" I had a shed constructed to protect the covered well and pumps. I also had a bench built inside on which to meditate. When it was finished it was a drab brown color that blended into the tree trunks of the surrounding area.

I hosted a gathering with many friends, one of whom had a profound experience during a meditation in which I invited people to find any spot on the 28 acres of MoonBear Sanctuary. My dear friend had been led to the water shed. When she was on the bench inside the water shed, she met an entity who called herself the Blue Water Goddess, although she said that wasn't her real name and that her name was too holy to reveal. The Blue Water Goddess said she wanted to be liberated, to be set free. She had been imprisoned for eons of time. She wanted the brown shed painted blue on the next blue moon. I contacted my handyman who came with his son to paint the shed a light blue on the New Blue Moon just a few days later. The Blue Water Goddess wanted blue river rock stones lining the sides of the dirt road leading to the shed. She also wanted to have gorgeous crystals and wind chimes hanging to bring beautiful sound to the area. We did all of this for her with love.

Later, I invited a wonderful group of my heart sisters to celebrate my birthday at a painting party for the Blue Water Goddess Temple, as the shed was christened in its new form. First, we said prayers and then everything unfolded in a miraculous way. Mariah, the woman who had met The Blue Water Goddess, was a talented artist who painted a huge mermaid with angel wings and ocean waves below her. Above the mermaid was a gigantic rainbow and a happy bright yellow and orange sun. All of the women invited jumped in and began painting. "Temple of the Blue Water Goddess" in beautiful lettering was hand-painted right at the front entrance. There was a huge whale taking up one whole side and ocean waves as well as musical notes. The Blue Water Goddess Temple had been painted into being with so much fun and love. Later that afternoon we continued my birthday celebration with a delicious mermaid birthday cake!

MoonBear property was large and had a lake within walking distance; there was an area where wild blackberries grew along a steep bank. I was out for a walk and couldn't resist picking some of them. Some of the riper berries were out of reach and while stretching to pick them I fell. Luckily, I was in jeans and a long-sleeved shirt, but the palms of my hands and wrists got cut. I returned to my house and cleaned up. As I lounged outside on my deck overlooking the beautiful forest view I noticed the shape of the Mystic Cross on not only one, but both of the palms on my hands. It is a very rare marking, also referred to as the Magician's M. In a Divine feminine circle, I was told it is the mark of the Mother Goddess. In the sunlight I noticed that the cuts on my palms went from just inside the left vertical line of the M to exactly the inside of the other vertical line of the M. It was perfectly situated, connecting both lines of the M. I found this to be absolutely fascinating. The cuts were more than an inch long. Strangely enough, as I was sitting in the sunshine looking at the cut on my left hand, I noticed that the cut line within the M had totally disappeared. Not a trace. Yet on my right hand, the cut would take 10 days to heal.

The following week, when I met with my Shamanic Astrologer, he said, "Kathleen, this time now is about the Heart of the Mother awakening in you in a new way. You are in a spiritual initiation, expanding and awakening to the truth of the Fierce Goddess and how she lives in the heart of the Mother. This is about the wild courageous bold kind of woman. It would be very powerful and beneficial to do a ceremony on June 29, the day this all kicks in astrologically. This initiation window of the Mother Awakening in you will last until March. If the heart of the mother could speak to you this is what she would say, "Kathleen, this is my truth and this is the way the fierce goddess you are experiences my truth and expresses it back out to the world. You are here to be a trailblazer, so that my heart awakens in you and others can follow this trail of the Mother's Heart. My heart is healing more every day. There is a responsibility to go into dark crevices of the Mother's heart and shine a light and love to all those dark places. Feel the pain of her broken heart. Broken-hearted mother energy. Her heart awakens in us. Have the courage to experience the pain and woundedness of the Mother's heart. Experience that pain. There is potential for a huge awakening in you, Kathleen.'"

On June 29 to acknowledge the Mother in my life I began to paint a picture of a great big heart, my heart with the Mother's heart awakening in the core of my heart. It had rays emanating out of the heart and also green leaves. That evening, I would participate in a ceremony of the Grandmother Ayahuasca. How amazing this ceremony would be in place and in perfect alignment for me to do a ceremony for acknowledging the energy and essence of the Mother and her awakening in my heart and in my life. During the ceremony I would remember being the Divine Goddess, waking up from the illusion of forgetting my divinity. I would feel deep gratitude for all the people who had played the characters in my "life movie." My ex-husband and the all-powerful male game he played with me. My son, Ben, and his love and his patience with me. The part my mother played for me. How perfectly my father had played his role, he could get an Academy Award. All these people were there to help wake me up from this dream. I was getting to see all of this from the perspective of unlimited Source and not just from the limited third-dimensional reality. Waking fully, remembering being Goddess creating this game of forgetting. Awakening fully to remember. I said to the shamanic facilitator "I remember. I see you. I love you. I see myself as Love awakening to Love."

I had many rituals and ceremonies at MoonBear Sanctuary, and one especially had the intention to awaken each woman's self-authenticating experience of wholeness and restoration. We held the first part, a water ritual with twelve women entering the hot tub one at a time while Mariah and I would guide and support each woman. As each woman would enter the water Mariah would energetically cut their cords with a large imaginary sword, severing any attachments and entrapments so they could go fully forward into the world with their holy work and embrace their highest vibration. This was a rite done in ancient times by Priestesses to keep the womb clean energetically. What we do individually for ourselves we also do for the whole of humanity. Some women cried, others screamed and some broke into heart-wrenching songs.

The second part of the ceremony was to honor the Blue Water Goddess and took place at her temple. She had conveyed that it was time for her liberation. After the ritual I realized we couldn't have chosen a more perfect day than Mother Mary's name day of September 12th.

A few weeks later I was kayaking on the lake by my home. This was the first year in the ten years I had lived there that river otters were on the lake. The symbolic meaning of otter is the Divine Feminine! I also saw a cinnamon-colored bear. I rescued a dragonfly that looked dead in the water. However, after I breathed warm air on it for 15 minutes, it suddenly shuddered and flew away. Dragonfly medicine is about change around perceptions of self-realization, going deeper to what is real, removing old limiting beliefs and living fully in the present moment!

Another ritual was with one of my significant totems, the eagle. There is an indigenous story of an eagle flying with only the right wing of the masculine. The left wing, symbolic of the feminine essence, had been broken, so the bird was flying in circles and couldn't fly straight. I had made a bird from clay and had taken it to the kiln a few days prior to the ceremony but the left wing broke off shortly before our ritual! I reattached the left wing to the bird with ceramic glue, and we all said prayers, seeing in our minds' eye the eagle now soaring everywhere with both her wings intact. It was a powerful and beautiful ceremony. Upon completion of this ritual, we saw that the eagle was now free and whole and complete, flying powerfully with both wings. Shortly after that I had a two-hour in-depth consultation with my homeopathic doctor who prescribed eagle medicine for me, made from an eagle whose left wing had been broken. I thought of the ritual I had just done and the significance of my totems once more.

So many amazing workshops were taking place at MoonBear Sanctuary: Transformational Breath Work with the founder Judith Kravitz; a two-week workshop of honoring the masculine and feminine led by Joseph and Elizabeth Sera from England; Aletheia Pistis Sophia held a Womb Wisdom workshop; midwifery was taught there; we also had Cellular Memory Release; and Family Constellations, to name a few more. There were also sacred plant journeys with Ayahuasca led by trained facilitators.

I led sacred journeys with women into Ecuador to the rainforest for the Pachamama Alliance. I would co-lead sacred journeys to Peru and to Guatemala with a person who lived in the respective country. I went with the author Jean Shinoda Bolen and a group of women to the United Nations conference for women.

I went on a fact-finding mission with some of the Nobel Women Peace Laureates to Israel and Palestine. We met with a large group of Israeli and Palestinian women. It is amazing what can be accomplished when women get together and talk and listen with our hearts, rather than in the masculine way — from our heads. When it finished I wanted to spend a little more time in the area. I was looking through my guidebook when it slipped out of my hands onto the floor, opening to "The Jesus Trail." The trail starts in Nazareth and ends in Galilee. After I outfitted myself with sturdy hiking boots and a good shade hat, I found myself in Israel alone. This was a little-known trail with complete solitude for me to walk. At one point I was lost along the border between Palestine and Israel. I was walking in circles, and it was getting close to sunset. I ran into a man who asked me if I needed help, and although I felt some trepidation to get into the huge shiny black SUV with this very large armed man who looked a bit ominous, he was my only option. He turned out to be a truly kind man who took me to a place to stay and recalibrate my journey along that path.

I have also had the good fortune to go on a sacred journey with just one or two friends, which is equally wonderful. Once, on a trip to Greece with my girlfriend, Mariah, we held a ceremony with a now-defunct Nuclear Bomb Key that was given to my ex-husband by a former United States Secretary of Defense in an unexpected regard of notable service Richard had given. I thought it was strange that this key would resurface after our being divorced for years. It suddenly appeared one day on top of my bookshelf. It was a key made of pewter in a strange cross-like shape, fat with rounded edges; it felt creepy in my hands. This had symbology to me, of the lower vibrational masculine that runs amok and creates division, war, and destruction.

I couldn't think of a more powerful ceremony other than to take it to Greece and release it into nature. My friend and I found the perfect location, a deep crevice within a cave we had hiked to. We deposited it there and held prayers for wholeness, love, peace, respect, and liberation for humanity, especially the feminine. We used a Palo Santo purification incense stick and blessed this site with full moon waters, moon-infused pearls, a white stone with a snake face I had found, and ceremonial oils gifted to me by a wonderful friend. This all took place on the fall equinox, an especially potent time to do sacred work. According to Sadhguru, the equinox is seen as a day when one has the best possibility of transcending the limitations and compulsions of one's physical longings. And masculine and feminine energies are on an even keel on this day.

We also did rituals and ceremonies at different sacred caves for the flourishing of the Divine Feminine on our planet. On one of our last days in Greece we visited the Temple of Athena and said prayers of gratitude where we were surrounded, actually blanketed, by hundreds of honeybees crawling all over our bodies including on our faces, on our eyelids. I told them I was allergic to them, and "if you must sting me, you have my permission." Only a moment later they all flew away. It was a trip focused around the Divine Feminine and her restoration on our planet. What a powerful affirmation, the significance of the bees relates to the goddess energy, respect for the power of the feminine, and the Divine Feminine.

Guatemala was another tour I co-led with a local Guatemalan woman who was steeped in the sacred wisdom of the Mayan elders. We had a small group of wonderful women, on the "Roar of the Jaguar" journey. One of the highlights about this nearly four-week journey was putting ourselves in Tikal with Mayan Elders on winter solstice, December 21, 2011. Tikal is a Mayan site in the Guatemalan jungle built between 700 BC and 900 AD. It is considered the most impressive of all the pre-Columbian sites in South America. In Mayan the name means "the place of the spirit voices". This particular trip focused around the 20-day Mayan calendar; the Jaguar as the animal or totem of the second chakra which represents sexuality and creativity, and the throat chakra which focuses on expression of our voice. It was an amazing journey; where our desires to be with shamans and to learn and experience the energies of the Mayan Calendar were fulfilled. We were so fortunate to have the opportunity to tour beautiful local villages and visit sacred Mayan sites. We visited caves with candlelit altars, beautiful riverbanks in the remote thick jungle, ending the journey on beaches of the Pacific Ocean where we saw a sea turtle laying eggs. My friend ran over and drew a circle around the eggs in the sand. That meant they had been claimed and no one could touch them. They were now safe.

The following year I led another journey to Peru with a very dear Peruvian friend. I knew that leading women to South America would be successful, exciting, life-changing and highly transformational for all of us. A couple of nights before the journey started, I was sleeping on my screened-in porch in Nevada City which I did in the summers. Sleeping outside under the moon and stars in fresh air was something I loved to do. This night in particular I was awakened by a large thud and what sounded like scraping nails and fierce growling. A huge bear had come onto the porch and was on its hind legs just on the other side of the thin screen that separated me and the bear. I leapt out of bed to face the bear, and in my fiercest voice commanded it to turn around and leave, which it immediately did. Yet I realized it hadn't gone far, I heard its rhythmic breathing nearby and with that, I found comfort and sleep again.

Strangely, the next day my sister and a very dear friend both called me to share dreams they had about me and a big bear. My sister had a dream that we were sitting on her front lawn eating blueberry cobbler fresh out of her oven, when a bear walked by us on the road. I insisted that we share some blueberry cobbler with the bear. My videographer friend called to say he had a dream of me and a bear. A huge bear had appeared and I asked if I could jump on my friend's back to walk past it. Interestingly in real life I jumped and faced the bear but sometimes I think caring men feel they need to protect women from something wild. Once again, the bear showed up in my life, symbolizing strength, vitality, and courage — just before the journey to Peru.

I sit here with the realization of how my life experiences brought me to this moment of understanding that I now embody the strength, vitality, and courage of the bear.

The most amazing women joined me for this journey. I flew to Peru first to visit with the friend with whom I was leading the trip, and then the women joined us at her home close to Cusco, a picturesque city. That evening we held the opening ceremony to initiate and bless this journey. It included items like charms, bundles of prayers, and seeds which are then burned in a sacred fire called a "Despacho," a ritual performed by Q'uero elders. This tour of Peru was designed to be one of both our inner and outer landscapes.

We visited many sacred sites on that trip, including Machu Picchu where we were all stunned by the immensity of the mountains and Incan rock buildings – an absolutely magical day there. Then on to a couple of other mountain villages, taking us to many Incan fortresses along the Urubamba River. Ollantaytambo, the village we would stay in to visit the various sacred sites of the Incans, was also the site of a massive fortress with large stone terraces built into the hillside.

Then onto The Sun Temple, Princess Baths Fountain, and Aguas Calientes where we stayed for the Full Moon. We all did a writing exercise on Our Warrior Selves and what gets in our way of becoming that person. We hiked to waterfalls where we would all experience release of the old and our new energies coming in. I remember that we each at some point had a butterfly or two land on us individually. We then gathered around an altar that was near a pool of water taking turns calling out our prayers then jumping into the freezing cold, clear mountain water. I yelled, "I am a warrior woman!" Clouds had built up while we were all taking claim to our prayers and when we had finished, a nearby bird sang, lightning struck, and thunder boomed. It was absolutely amazing for all of us.

Upon returning to our originating village, we had our Closing Ceremony, thanking the Divine Feminine, all the inner and outer work we had undertaken, and then eating deliciously blessed food made for us with love as part of our sacred travels. A dear girlfriend and I remained in Peru to go to Lake Titicaca, then Aramu Muru. I was told what an amazing experience it would be to journey there. She was sick in bed the next day so I traveled with a guide and a driver to Aramu Muru.

Aramu Muru is a large flat stone with a T-shaped niche forming a doorway with streaks of white and red mineral deposits on either side of it. It is a portal, according to legend, that allowed Inca priests to be transported to different places of the Inca Empire and even to any place in the world. The inter-dimensional gate Aramu Muru, also known as Hayu Marca, means City of Spirits or Willka Uta: "Place of the sun or gate of the gods."

The red rocks reminded me of the Canyonlands National Park in the USA, large rock structures with sacred sites everywhere. As we began walking to Amaru Muru, a baby white hawk with a red tail began circling over our heads. We hiked farther to the wall. The driver had driven around and was waiting on the road. My guide went to the car for her singing bowls. I sat on the ground on a flat stone, level with the earth and facing the wall. My guide then began playing the singing bowls and I had a chrysocolla gemstone, a condor feather, and a red Tibetan stone in my hands and the Priestess Stone was wrapped in a cloth tied to my body at my waist. I began deep meditation, and I immediately dropped into a very ancient time. I was the High Priestess at a temple for priestesses. There were carved stone bathing pools. I was in beautiful warm waters. Other priestesses were caring for me. They were bathing me and anointing me with sacred oils on my chakras, even the chakras on the bottoms of my feet and the palms of my hands. They dried me off and dressed me in a fine thin, linen-like robe. They were preparing me. At the same time, my masculine counterpart was also being prepared. Then I was taken to a bridal chamber. There was my beloved but more in a spiritual realm. We were united and came together, making love. Then a voice asked if I was ready and I said, "Yes, this is the time and the place, and I am prepared."

We were in ancient Lemuria and my Peruvian friend was with me. We were the high Priest and High Priestess of that civilization. We were extremely tall beings. We were facing the Stargate wall together and through his intentions he made the masculine indent and white streak in the rock wall, and though my intention I made the feminine indent with a red streak. He was the Masculine Christ, and I was the Feminine Christ. Joining in my vision were others holding sacred energies of the Feminine Christ and Masculine Christ. Directions were taken by the Feminine Christ energies, bringing together the polarities of masculine and feminine, old and young, hot and cold, night and day, sun and moon, good and bad, etc. We flew through the cosmos around planets and the red planet, Mars.

I then went to the white masculine indent on the right side of the Stargate and stood there for many minutes with my arms raised, being infused with the masculine energies. I could feel this masculine energy running through me. I then walked to the place of the red feminine energies and stood in the indent on the left side of the Stargate with my arms raised. I then proceeded to the Stargate Doorway, and instead of kneeling I knew I was to squat with my feet planted firmly on the ground. Inside the doorway is an indentation where I was directed to place my third eye. Before taking that position, I placed my "k'intu," which is made of three coca leaves and prayers on the ground as an offering. I had also brought a bottle of gold from Nevada City, and I said a prayer for forgiveness for all the violence and stealing of gold from Peru by the Spanish invaders and the knowing that the real gold was not physical but one of consciousness.

I then took my position, squatting with feet firmly planted on the earth, with hands raised up on the wall and my third eye at the hole. Immediately a baby came through me and was born and then it was wrapped in a blanket and handed to me. I was surprised it came out so quickly, easily, and so fast. It was not a physical baby but the birth of the Golden Age of love, light, and peace. All the Gods and Goddesses were smiling and saying "YES!" It was a success!

I arrived back at my hotel room absolutely exhausted. My girlfriend, with whom I was staying, looked at me and said, "You look like you have just birthed a baby!!" I crawled into my bed; it was 5 p.m. and I slept until morning! It is interesting because a few months before my journey to Peru I had had visions of a baby coming through me. I was so close to this baby's birth that its head was crowning. Then I heard a voice say, "STOP! This isn't the time or the place." Now I knew why! It needed to take place at the Stargate Amaru Muru.

I recently met a woman in Sedona who is an authority on Amaru Muru. She said the man Amaru Muru, whom this Stargate is named after, appears as a white hawk. So now I know he was with me there at Amaru Muru — the white hawk circling me as I approached the portal and the whole time I was there!!

CHAPTER TWELVE

RETURNING TO NEVADA CITY

In Nevada City, at MoonBear Sanctuary, many other things were taking place. I presided over "blessing way" ceremonies for mothers-to-be, making them wreaths from roses from my garden and offering foot baths with essential oils. Prayers and poems from their sacred sisters would shower them with love and blessings.

One of my friends, Josie Stein, led hypnosis journeys; one of her clients was author Wayne Dyer. She had a phenomenal reputation around the work she did. A group of dear friends gathered at MoonBear where we all found out we were from the Jesus tribe. My connection was Mother Mary. After that I started a daily practice for many years, channeling her.

Also, at this time a lot of healing work was taking place in my life as I was working with a therapist weekly, as well as a somatic trauma therapist. Each month I would drive nearly four hours to Strozzi Institute in Petaluma, in Northern California for a four-hour session with Staci Haines, the author of *Healing Sex: a Mind Body Approach* to *Healing Sexual Trauma*. It was intense! We started with talking therapy and then she would take me into somatic healing ... right into my body as I was lying on a massage table. Touching areas that hold trauma. Memories would come up. It was so freaking intense to do the work and face the traumas and wounds. I would then have the long, four-hour drive home ... I would pass Whole Foods on the highway and get something to eat, sitting outside at a wooden table, writing in my journal, writing my experiences of what had shown up during the healing session. We did this month after month. But still, I was not healed.

One day I realized that even if I did a billion hours of healing and talking therapy, there would never come a day when suddenly all those traumas and wounds were gone ... like erasing a tape. But maybe with all that work (and this makes me cry), I stretched myself big enough that I was able to hold all the horror that happened to me. Hold it all with love. It was never deleted but somehow through all the work I had become big enough to hold it and the charge was no longer there. It was no longer a live wire. I was no longer acting and reacting to the wounds. It was gone. I was now love awakening to love.

I have learned to be more gentle with myself. More accepting. To listen to what my body wants, what my heart wants, what lights me up. I sometimes still get attracted to the wrong kind of man, but my friends can point that out to me.

Living at my retreat center in Nevada City I felt seen, I felt loved for just who I was. Who I was not only was enough, but it was also valued and appreciated. I was authentically me and I loved so dearly all my wonderful, amazing friends and all the incredible people I would meet living there.

Another big shift in my life began in 2018 with a voice class on the Shift Network with musician, performer, and songwriter Chloe Goodchild. I contacted her to do some private sessions with me. She was in London, and I was in Nevada City. We did our sessions on Zoom.

She asked me to make up a song and sing it to her. I told her there was a song I always heard in my head that I would sometimes sing, "I and the Mother are one, under the moon and under the sun; I and the Mother are one are one, I and the Mother are one." She got all excited and ran out of her room and came back with a huge image in a beautiful frame of Anandamayi Ma, Divine Mother from India who crossed over in August, 1992. Once I glanced at her I couldn't stop weeping. I wept for days. All I knew was that I had to go to India and find her even though she was no longer in her body. I had a deep desire to let go of everything I owned and to go to India and live simply in devotion to the Divine Mother for the rest of my life.

After completing a Sufi Sesshin, a retreat that combines sitting meditation with the Dances of Universal Peace, for a week in Northern California there was a talk about how they were raising money for a Dargah, a sacred statue, in New Mexico in memory of Murshid Samuel Lewis. I felt the Divine tap me on my shoulder and whisper "Give your five acres of land on the Ocean with huge rocks and crashing waves in Elk, Mendocino County, California to the Sufi's." So I did.

I decided to sell my home in Nevada City and to give all my physical possessions away. I called it "The Great Giveaway." I gathered all my nice kitchen things, nearly all of my clothing which I actually sold to raise money for an organization to empower women.

I then invited 15 close girlfriends and we had a sacred circle before my giveaway to my community. They took control and placed me in the center. They each shared qualities they most admired about me. They spoke about how they appreciated all I had done and showered me with blessings and prayers for moving forward on my path to India.

As the ceremony completed, the rest of my friends and community arrived for the giveaway. I had placed my books, clothing, some art, and all kinds of possessions like kayaks and bikes which I dearly loved, as well as golf clubs from my previous life of being married, out for the women to take. I gave my sister, Patti, some of my favorite art that I loved and some handwoven rugs, I gave her husband my Toyota Tundra truck. My brother got my Lexus, he was just moving back from living overseas for many years and needed a car. Sacred statues of deities went to dear friends. After selling my home and sanctuary I drove a U-Haul with my handwoven rugs I had collected from around the world as well as most of my art to give to my mother in Salt Lake City, Utah.

All I knew was that I had to find Anandamayi Ma and planned to live simply in India in meditation doing Nam Japa, a mantra with my mala beads and doing seva (service work) for the rest of my life.

Pir Shabda Khan, the head of the Sufi Ruhaniat order who had recently led the Mendocino Sufi Sesshin that I had attended, talked to me, and asked me if I had met a man named Mangalanda who had been at the Sesshin. I hadn't. He and his wife lived close enough they were commuting. He gave me his contact information and he told him I would be reaching out to him. It was a Sunday and raining hard in Mill Valley where I was staying in a dear friend's guest quarters, an apartment above their garage. It was late afternoon when I emailed Mangalananda. He responded, inviting me to an event that evening he was leading with kirtan and talks about Anandamayi Ma, about 20 minutes north of where I was staying. I drove in torrential rain to get there. That evening there was even an eclipse! Afterward, he made an announcement that he would be leading a trip to India. I asked if I could join them, but it was fully booked, and all arrangements had been made. He said he would meet me and help me plan my trip.

As soon as he sat down at the cafe Book Passages in Corte Madera, he told me he could not say no to me. I was supposed to be on this trip. When Mangalananda was 18 he had spent a year with Anandamayi Ma in India before she crossed over!

I had bought a one-way, non-refundable plane ticket booked to India and would arrive there three weeks before he and his group would arrive.

CHAPTER THIRTEEN

INDIA

On my journey to India, my heart was filled with complete renunciation of worldly things and a deep commitment to living the rest of my life in service to the purity of love I experienced when I first saw Anandamayi Ma's image and cried for days. My heart was pierced and there was no turning back.

To my surprise and dismay, I discovered my desire and the reality in India ". . . was the best of times and it was the worst of times." As in the beginning of A Tale of Two Cities.

Upon landing in India in January 2019, I immediately knew I was someplace quite different. India is colorful, and women wear the most beautiful sari's, often of bright, stunning colors. Even women whose work is cleaning homes will be wearing a sari to do so.

Cows are revered, they represent the Mother, as it is a source of goodness, and its milk nourishes all creatures. They are considered to be like mothers. Mothers give their babies milk, which is one of the most important things for growing up and being healthy. Krishna, an important and revered deity in India, was a cowherd. It is common to see cows walking on a major motorway and everything comes to a stop until the cows have passed by. This is simply part of the rhythm of what makes up India.

Drinking chai is an integral part of India. I love the taste of Indian chai with crushed up cardamom pods infusing the taste, along with other rich spices. Morning starts with chai for breakfast. And at 4 p.m. people take a break to drink afternoon chai. It is served in a small cup and savored, not the giant-sized American coffee cup! It is a ritual observed in every part of India that I visited, and I loved this ritual.

India is noisy. There is music, dancing, laughter. A wedding can last several days, and it is common for the music to play all night over gigantic loudspeakers while the participant's dance. Cars honk on narrow roads while going around blind curves to let oncoming cars become aware they are there. In America, if you visit a home where there is a newborn baby you are expected to whisper so as not to disturb or wake up the baby. In India I witnessed babies sleeping through all situations and noise levels. The notion that it has to be quiet to sleep does not exist in India. India is filled with sound and smells. Cars are constantly honking, with music blaring. I often would see someone sound asleep in the middle of surrounding chaos and loud noise; totally unaffected by it all.

Everywhere I went in India the people were so friendly, wanting to say "hello" and to speak a few words of English with me. Everyone was always so helpful, especially in pointing out directions for me.

My first intention upon arriving in India was to detox, receive healing treatments, continue yoga and meditation, and change my diet to adjust to the new life on which I was embarking. After two weeks of staying in Rishikesh at the Veda 5 Ayurvedic Center, I was ready to leave with my group, led by Mangalananda, a man who was one of the last people on the planet to have spent time with Anandamayi Ma. I was so fortunate to have our paths cross and to take such a small intimate tour with only five of us, plus Mangalananda and his wife, Gloria, as we traveled together to a few different ashrams of AnandaMayi Ma's in Dehradun, Haridwar and Vrindavan.

After Vrindavan, the last Anandamayi Ma ashram we visited was MaSharanam, close to the banks of the Narmada River in Central India. It had a school for children from surrounding towns, an ashram for boys, and dorms for visiting spiritual devotees. It was suggested by Mangalananda that I might want to continue living there. He had helped to found this amazing center of devotion to Anandamayi Ma. SwamiJi and Sarabjeet ran the ashram. SwamiJi (Swami Gee) was the ashram's Swami, meaning master, a man who dedicates his life to a spiritual discipline or path, and his brother, Sarabjeet, was in charge of all the financials including acting as bookkeeper/accountant.

What a blessing; I was invited to stay at the ashram, and I did! The group I was traveling with departed, and my decision felt perfect. I quickly established my rhythm at the ashram. Waking up daily at 3:30 a.m. to do my spiritual practices in my room, I would use mala beads to do my Nama Japa, saying "OM MA" with each of the 108 beads. I read from spiritual texts for about an hour and a half. Then I would shower, dress, and prepare for the day.

I would go to the Mandir (temple), dedicated to Anandamayi Ma, the largest of the temples at the ashram. I would sweep and place fresh roses that I would gather from the gardens and put in front of a bust of Anandamayi Ma. This meditation, of sweeping and offering roses, was given to me as part of my daily Seva, service work.

When I first got to the ashram SwamiJi and nearly everyone at the ashram addressed me as Mother, which was very honoring and respectful. Ghanshyam, who was an amazing healer and ran many activities to keep the ashram going, would not only address me as Mother but he would also pranam, lay flat on the ground before me. He was a Godsend placed in my life, as he was also a phenomenal healer. He kept me taped together while living at the ashram. His beautiful wife, Gayatri, was my friend and we tried to learn to play the harmonium together although I can't say that was successful. Their son, Samrat, who was about 3 ½, was so sweet and would come to my room to watercolor with me, or we would walk to the Narmada together to skip rocks. Later, he had a little sister come into the world, named Simran.

Starting at 6 a.m. each day as part of the devotion to Anandamayi Ma and living at the ashram, everyone would assemble for morning practice, songs, and Arati – the custom of using a small brass dish, which looks very similar to a lit Genie lamp, which would be used in a circular motion at the altar in reverence to Ma. I remember the sounds we had at the ashram, with the harmonium playing devotional songs. We would then move to the outdoor area with an altar devoted to Radha Krishna where SwamiJi would read from Anandamayi Ma's book "The Essential Sri Anandamayi Ma; Life and Teachings of a 20th century Saint from India." Every day, this time was used for spiritual lessons for the boys who lived at the ashram. SwamiJi would ask questions to ensure the boys understood Anandamayi Ma's teachings.

Then we would proceed as a group to the Temple of Ganesha, a larger building to accommodate the yoga asanas we would practice there. Kali Mandir was last, and the only ceremony led by the ashram's Pandit, a Hindu priest trained in Holy Vedic Scripture. It was a small temple, enough to hold a square fire pit. There would usually be SwamiJi and a few other adults including myself. We would toss seeds into the fire saying, "Swaha." We were throwing them into the fire to let go of anything in our life we are ready to release. It is also a chant in oblation to Kali. At the ashram, all the temples were built in a circular design, whereas the other buildings – dorms, houses, and the cafeteria — were built in the western rectangular style.

All of the devotion would take place in two hours, because breakfast was promptly served at 8 a.m. We would sit in chairs outside, and we mostly had the same breakfast of Poha – a flattened, par-boiled rice that was easily made for many people. We would occasionally have fruit like papaya or bananas, and of course the delicious chai. I would usually get a second helping of that.

After eating breakfast, the left-overs were taken to the enclosure for the cows where they would be fed and brushed. Following that, I had my daily Seva (service work) of peeling and chopping vegetables for meal preparations. At sunset we would have Aarti again in Ma's temple and sometimes we would do devotion right on the banks of the Narmada River. It was extremely beautiful witnessing the setting sun.

The man at the ashram who took care of the cows at the "Goshala," an enclosure for cows, invited me to his home to meet his wife. She made an incredible lunch for me. Also, the man who built furniture and other things at the ashram wanted me to meet his family, taking me there on his motorcycle. They also had a delicious lunch for me. I love Indian food and it was such a gift to be welcomed into their homes.

Sometimes in the afternoon, the boys would play volleyball with SwamiJi. SwamiJi is a large man, I would estimate 6'5" with large bones and is very substantial. The boys were younger, early teens, and on the small side. One day I was watching them play. One of the boys on the opposing team had made a play where SwamiJi had hit the ball into the net, giving the boys' team a point. The boy who had just made this point did a short victory dance. SwamiJi reacted in anger, yelling and berating this boy. SwamiJi had a temper that would occasionally flare up.

If I ever needed to go to the city Indore, Sarabjeet and his wife Shruti would lovingly open up their home for me to stay in with their two amazingly kind children in their teens as well as MommiJi and PapaJi, their parents. PapaJi was a homeopathic doctor and never charged anyone for his services. Both Sarabjeet and Shruti are amazing cooks. Shruti would always make me parathas, my favorite breakfast, which is similar to a pancake but not sweet.

I began to study Hindi. Learning a language in general was never easy for me and Hindi was especially difficult because I had to learn a whole new alphabet in new symbols of Hindi lettering. I also went to a Hindi language school in Jaipur for a few weeks in April after I had been in India for a few months, so that I could study Hindi and get the basics down. Both Nani, who was from France and lived half the year at the ashram and half in France, and also MommiJi, the mother of SwamiJi and Sarabjeet, would help me with my Hindi, but for the amount of effort they put in, my Hindi barely improved.

Upon completing my two weeks of Hindi lessons in Jaipur and celebrating my birthday there, I flew to Dharamasala. I met up with SwamiJi and a few boys who were already staying at the small second ashram they owned and had a mandir (temple), to Anandamayi Ma as well as a kitchen and a small sleeping area. It was beautiful, with huge mountains surrounding us, and hawks soaring overhead. There wasn't a sleeping area for me, so I stayed at a homestay a few miles away and would come early in the morning and leave after dinner. In the afternoon SwamiJi would lovingly have one of the boys prepare a space for me to take my afternoon nap. A tuk-tuk, a small three-wheeled vehicle, would take me there each morning and be there to pick me up in the early evening. I would help with cutting vegetables for meal preparation. I also cleaned and washed all the windows and washed all the white curtains in Ma's Mandir, with the help of Mahesh, one of the boys there with SwamiJi.

Anandamayi Ma's birthday came around on April 30th. Many people who were part of the Anandamayi Ma family community arrived at this ashram for the amazing celebration, and what a beautiful celebration it was. We had a gigantic pile of rose petals that had been heaped up over several feet long in front of us. What a beautiful sight and smell. We used these rose petals to toss into the center in a ceremony that lasted a very long time in reverence to her. Later there were harmoniums playing and lots of singing. I felt like I was in seventh heaven. We then feasted, and what a feast it was. I have to say we had the most amazing cooks at the ashram. Every bite was heavenly. And the food was prepared with "bhav" which might translate to a feeling of love or reverence. Being present to the food and what you are doing while preparing it is important, as those feelings transfer into the food.

From there a group of us traveled to the Golden Temple, which is made of 24-karat gold. This is a sacred temple for Sikhs, as SwamiJi and Sarabjeet's family were Sikhs. It is located in the holy city of Amritsar which is one of the most gorgeous places on Earth. It is run by people showing up to do seva (service) preparing food, serving food, or cleaning up dishes and washing. We also volunteered our time to do seva there.

That summer when it got hot in India, I followed SwamiJi to Europe and attended workshops he was leading there with followers of Anandamayi Ma. We went to Germany and to Austria, then I went by myself to Stockholm, Sweden, to visit my son and his lovely partner, Cecilia; I had a fabulous time with them. They took me indoor rock climbing and, although it was my first time at it, I was a natural, instantly enjoyed it and wished I had been introduced to the sport earlier in my life! There was a reason I once had the nick-name of "monkey!"

In September, shortly after returning to India, I went to Almora, a picturesque hill-station surrounded by pine and oak forests to stay at one of the ashrams of Anandamayi Ma. She had spent time there and had a bedroom there. It still had some of her items. The Swami and I would go into her room to do our evening meditations. There were also monkeys all around, so the Swami gave me a stick to carry around in case one tried to jump on me. We had a joke about my "monkey stick." I visited many incredible sites while I was there. My favorite was the Katarmal Sun Temple which is more than 800 years old and well known for its intricate sculptures.

From there I met Sarabjeet and Shruti and their two children at the Golden Temple where we spent a few days before returning to Indore and then the ashram for me. SwamiJi did a solo journey, walking the Narmada Parikrama; departing on December 16 and returning February 5th. I had been secretly told he was walking it in search of a deep question and wanting clarity. Before I arrived at the ashram, he had fallen in love with a European woman visiting there. I was told he had come to the crossroads of needing to decide if he would carry on as the Swami of the ashram or marry her. She was the same woman he stayed with in her house on our European trip. This was part of the hypocrisy that began to bother me. Our pandit, which basically means Priest, had fallen in love with a beautiful European woman who was staying at the ashram and had wanted to marry her. He had taken her to his village to meet his parents and family. After his shoes were seen outside of her ashram room, he was kicked out of the ashram. All of his belongings were thrown onto the pavement while Sarabjeet was screaming and yelling at him and saying he could never set foot in the ashram again. What is this double standard, I wondered.

In mid-February, 2020, I flew to Sri Lanka for a visa run. I could only be in India for six months at a time. Upon landing and departing the plane there were all kinds of signs asking if you had a fever and a whole long table stacked with pamphlets. This was the first time I became aware of Covid. Shortly after returning to the ashram the school had to close down and all the boys except for a few went home to their families. I would coach the few boys still at the ashram with their English studies. One day SwamiJi wouldn't let me continue; I never knew why.

When I first arrived at the ashram the year before, I was handed a flyer proposing building a girls' dorm. The costs were planned at $30,000 USD for completion, and I wanted to see the girls thriving and empowered in a safe environment to grow. I offered to pay the 30K and felt great about my decision to help and commit to gifting this money. Shortly after gifting it, Sarabjeet told me they were NOT going to be building a girl's dorm, yet he asked me where I would like my donation to go. I wanted the money to go to the kids and told him specifically that this money should go to the boys. Many months passed after I made the 30K USD donation for the children and in hindsight I don't think that the money going to the kids was ever part of their plan. I offered to make this donation because I love children and wanted to see them flourish. I never saw anything manifest from the money I had donated.

I asked to have a meeting with Sarabjeet and SwamiJi because I wanted to know where my donation was going. Sarabjeet saw me outside, in a cold, curt voice told me to go to my room immediately for the meeting. I could feel he was irritated with me. Sarabjeet, Shruti and SwamiJI and I met in my room. I asked where my large donation went and he said to a bank account that would make 6.5% interest, which felt strange that the money wasn't going to the places I wanted it to go. When I donated it, they had insisted I designate a place where the money would go. It didn't feel good to me to take money out of my bank and put it into his bank to make interest. I wanted it to go to the children, not a high interest-bearing bank account. I wanted the money to have a purpose, but I acquiesced, and didn't mention the money again. Shruti jumped up, hugging me and telling me how wonderful I was; however, I could feel how angry Sarabjeet and SwamiJi were. From that point on, there would always be a rift between us. There was a coldness. It wasn't spoken but it was definitely felt. My questioning about the money I donated was ultimately my undoing of me living there.

There were multiple instances in which I was suddenly not included in events or happenings. Previously, I would have been included and gladly joined in. I had originally been told I was family there. Now everything shifted, and it felt awful to me. I had established a wonderful relationship with MommiJi, the mother of the brothers who ran the ashram. She spent many hours helping me learn Hindi as well as many hours peeling and chopping vegetables together doing seva. She and her husband were celebrating their 50th wedding anniversary in Indore where they lived at Sarabjeet and Shruti's home. She had personally invited me to their celebration although I didn't know the exact date. The afternoon of the event Sarabjeet had ordered a car to pick up two women who were visiting the ashram for a week from Europe but had left me behind. Later MommiJi asked why I had not attended. I told her the car had only been arranged for the other two women and I was not included.

Lots of things were coming to the forefront at the ashram, including continued problems with me asking where my donation had gone. Although I loved the ashram, things between myself and the brothers, SwamiJi and Sarabjeet, were disintegrating daily. Small and large snubs, from Sarabjeet, such as "forgetting" to place my Amazon order, to simply not including me in getting sweets given after lunch to everyone but me, even though we all had our hands cupped in front of us. Also having the Sikh Holy Book read for you in a deep prayer, you were wanting answered. My cost was $300. I later found out everyone else was charged $100.

The overcharge for my small house was a large abuse of money. It was at their suggestion that I had them build my own house. I was so touched that they wanted me to have a home there. That took longer and cost more than any other house at the ashram, three times more. My house was really just a rectangle with a bed at one end and an armoire next to it. It included a small puja table to do my Nam Japa, chanting with 108 mala beads, each morning. A table by the front window to eat at or study. With a small area on the side with a sink and hot plate and also a bathroom. They charged me $10,500. Again, three times the cost. They asked me for my final payment before it was finished and then took the workers off my house, delaying the finish by two months and put them to work on finishing the Sikh Mandir and upgrading the area for the cows.

I later found out Sarabjeet deceived me by overcharging for my visa extension. I found this out several months later when I called the visa officer who had previously come to the ashram to meet me. After that he was always doing what he could to help me. He said it had not been much, the only cost was the hired car and that had been approximately $330. Sarabjeet charged me $1000 USD. It was a never-ending situation in which I was always at the losing end of the circumstance. I felt so betrayed and taken advantage of. I continued to pray to Anandamayi Ma for help, surrendering everything to her.

I had a huge insight, an ashram in India is patriarchal even though we are devoted to AnandaMayi Ma. SwamiJi is head of the spiritual side which is as it should be. Sarabjeet is the head of the structure, running it, the money, things like telling me to pay for a hired car that was filled to the brim with huge bags of vegetables and I was squished against the door. It was clearly being used for the ashram's business. Once we arrived at the ashram, I had to start preparing all these vegetables.

I woke up one morning to this thought: "The truth shall set you free."

It was Republic Day ceremony, and I was invited to come along and celebrate. I was very surprised when SwamiJi gave me the honor of lighting the Aarti lamp. I was called up to the front to do this. Later that day I found out he wanted $2,000 USD from me to fund Vrindavan musicians to play non-stop music for an entire month for world peace. I gave him the money. And quickly, it reverted back to how it had been for months of being ignored and slighted. It was clear to me that money was the only motivation they had for my future at the ashram.

I found myself crying to sleep at night as I had when I was a child, knowing that the situation at the ashram was quickly deteriorating. Friends who were close were telling me how financially and emotionally mistreated I was there. I was returning to old patterns about self-worth and being enough. I knew something was wrong. I was trying everything I knew to improve the situation, but the coldness didn't end. I saw how my earlier traumas, abuse, and my childhood beliefs of if I can only be good enough, give enough, be kind and nice enough, I will be loved, accepted and appreciated. Anandamayi Ma came to me and I was compelled to come to India. Now I know this journey was necessary to reveal places inside of me that still needed to be healed. I came to India believing I had dealt with all of this, but what I have learned is there are layers upon layers upon layers. Our life journey continues to reveal where there are still places to heal and grow.

CHAPTER FOURTEEN

MY TRUE INDIA FAMILY

At the same time, I had found my true family of the heart and pure love in India. Neha came in like an angel, as my life story would always bring in support and guidance for my heart. Oddly, it was my dentist Neha who is beautiful and in her mid-twenties. I got my teeth cleaned by her every other month because we consumed so much sugar in India, which I don't usually eat. And it only cost $10 to get your teeth cleaned. And she would arrange for the local barber to come cut my short hair; that cost $1.50. After that she would bring me upstairs and her beautiful mother would serve me a fantastic lunch. Everything she cooked was delicious and done with love. Neha would walk me up to her bedroom. She would tell me to lie down on her bed, and she would cover me with a cozy blanket and tell me to take a nap. Naps are customary in India. She would come back an hour later and arrange for a ride back to the ashram for me.

One day after I had seen Neha to get my teeth cleaned, she said to me, "Kathleen, I know you are much older than I am, but I really like you. Can we become dear friends?" I replied, "I really like you too! Yes, of course! I would love that." So that is how our friendship started.

Her father was the local doctor for the whole area. He was also the doctor for the boys at our ashram. He charged people a fraction of the price and if they didn't have the money, he would treat them anyway. Once I stepped on a rusty nail and he came to the ashram and gave me a tetanus shot.

Neha took me to her neighbors and introduced me. We even went on a fun outing with her mother, best friend Aditi, and the little boy from next door to go to Maheshwar where they had the most gorgeous silk fabrics that we would have made into sari's. And we stopped for ice cream on the way home.

Her grandfather had died of Covid, and she invited me to be part of her family and go to his home and sit with the family, having dinner together. And then sitting on the floor while live music was playing and there was a photo of him, we were looking at. He had been cremated at a place along the Narmada River where they do that. It was such an honor and displayed such deep love that she would invite me to be part of this intimate ritual with her family.

When everything was falling apart at the ashram, her family wanted to go on a road trip to take me to Vrindavan. I dearly wanted to go there before leaving India. But at the last minute, because of Covid, we were not able to make that trip.

INSULT TO INJURY – PLANE TICKET HOME TO USA

On August 9th 2020 I was told I had to leave India because of Covid. Foreigners were going to be forced to leave India. I was told by Sarabjeet, Jasdeep, his brother-in-law who had a small travel agency had to put my $3500 business class ticket onto his credit card, as it needed to be issued by an Indian bank, and I had to XOOM, a way to transfer international funds, Jasdeep $3500 cash which I did. It actually turned out to be 7 months later in March that I flew out of Delhi to San Francisco and then to Salt Lake City, Utah. Before departing, Sarabjeet told me Jasdeep had spent $1500 of the cash I had sent to him and he didn't have it to pay me back so I needed to forgive him of this debt as there was no alternative. I remember seeing his family suddenly showing up with new clothing and all kinds of new things. Now, looking back I wish I would have taken a taxi to the police station. I am sure the $1500 would have turned up very quickly, after all Sarabjeet still had the $30,000, I had donated to the girls' ashram which was never built.

It turned out, I needed to leave India because my visa couldn't be extended. Looking back, I am curious if Sarabjeet had anything to do with it. I realized I had to do all my transactions through him. I wanted to believe I could trust Sarabjeet's words that I truly was family, but this was crazy-making. I was dismissed, deceived, taken advantage of, while I was being smiled at and told I was family. This is just like my father saying you're my daughter and then raping me. It was family then and it was awful.

Both situations were filled with polarities and deceit. What did that mean to them that I was family? It felt like they owned me and all they wanted was what served or benefited them. I am sitting in deep sadness remembering how bad the situation really was in India. Just like the little girl who thought if she did it right and gave from her heart, it would make things right with people. I realized it had to get this bad for me to wake up and see what was going wrong. From the outside the beauty of the ashram and the land was majestic, the ideal was what I aspired to. But in reality, it was a repeat of my initial imprints of being betrayed and abused by my father. When it came down to it, I didn't feel sad about leaving the ashram and India. Instead, I found myself in total surrender to what was happening. My prayer is to continue to see things more clearly as they are, not how I want them to be.

> "Betrayal is the ultimate act of cowardice.
> It takes courage to be honest.
> But it takes no courage to deceive.
> It is a choice. Not a mistake.
> It's a conscious decision to put
> self interest above loyalty and truth."
>
> Dr. Lucas D. Shall

This quote helps me to see I was the courageous one!

CHAPTER FIFTEEN

CARING FOR MY MOTHER

It was early evening when I landed at San Francisco International Airport coming back from India. I had received a call from my sister saying Mom had fallen and was in the hospital. I was the only one who could take care of her, so I needed to get on the next plane to Salt Lake City. Luckily, there was a room available at one of the closest airport hotels; it had the softest, most luxurious sheets, towels, and bathrobe. Also in the room was an espresso coffee machine. What a contrast to my life in India! I booked the flight to Salt Lake City for the following morning. Unfortunately, upon arriving in Salt Lake City airport, my Covid test was inconclusive, so my family wanted me to quarantine first. I found an upscale boutique hotel with a great room that was also known for their fantastic food and fabulous chef at their restaurant. The food was incredible.

By the time I was able to go to my mother's home she had been discharged from the hospital. Luckily, she did not have any broken bones. She had fallen in her kitchen and spent the night and most of the following day on the floor before a neighbor found her and she was admitted to the hospital. After I arrived, we had a home nurse, a physical therapist, and a nurse's aide showing up to check on her, work on her mobility, and wash her. What a strong woman to make it to 93 before needing assistance! Until her fall she was still driving and even after the fall she would play bridge and often win. She was sharp.

Unfortunately, when I arrived there was no car available to drive because my mom had a minor road accident in a construction zone, leaving her car with a small side scrape. The insurance company decided to total her low-mileage Lexus. She only got $500 for the car, and to me, it seemed like the insurance company was taking advantage of her at her age.

My sister Patti worked full-time, going into her job super early in the morning so she was free to take care of her granddaughters in the afternoons. She would drive 20 minutes to pick up Mom and me to take us to her doctor appointments.

One afternoon in a quiet moment I was standing in the kitchen at my mom's house, looking out the south-facing window, and a vision of an old friend, whom I had not seen for nearly 40 years, flashed into my mind. I did a little sleuthing and found Bill on Facebook.

He would come to my mother's house twice a week to take me hiking up Mill Creek Canyon. The start of the trailhead was a five-minute drive from her house. He and I had a limited amount of time together because I needed to care for my mom; but he was a God-Goddess send. It was a deep platonic friendship from our hearts and souls. He even found me a car so I could get my mother to all of her appointments. I was so grateful to reconnect with him because this was the same man who helped me move to California at age 27. He was the furthest person from my mind and yet here he was again, helping me in another major life transition.

At one of Mom's appointments, they had taken X-rays and found cancer in her uterus. Her doctor recommended she have an operation and have her uterus removed, telling her all the cancer was contained within her uterus. I did not think an operation at her age was a good idea, but she dearly loved her female doctor and wanted to do what she recommended. After the operation it was discovered that the cancer had not been contained in her uterus and was spreading. I think having a serious operation and being put under anesthesia at 93 years of age was greatly detrimental to her health and shortened her life span. They then put her in hospice and gave her morphine and fentanyl daily. When the doctor first mentioned hospice, I said, "How can my mom be in hospice care, she is so vibrant, and she isn't dying, and this service is only available for six months." I do believe the drugs accelerated her death.

One day there was an unexpected knock at my mother's front door. Bill was there! That was such a surprise because he never showed up unexpectedly. He felt called to come. As we both looked down, we saw a dead bird on her porch. He said he would bury it, which he did. When he came back and I opened the door there was a hummingbird fluttering right in front of us. I told him, Mom's totem is the hummingbird, she loves them with all her heart. I said "she will be dying very soon, you need to go. Thanks so much for tuning in and stopping by!" That was late afternoon.

I was sleeping each night on the sofa next to my mother's hospital bed in the living room, so I could be there if she needed anything. I can't explain why but I really wanted to be with her when she took her very last breath. Morning came and I was just standing up and starting to walk by mom when I heard the sound and knew it was her last breath. An angel intuitive later told me mom had communicated to her that the first thing she encountered as she left her body was my spirit and how beautiful that was to be there together as she transitioned. Then she was greeted by her parents and siblings on the other side who were so happy to have her with them.

Starting with her fall, cancer, and death, getting her house sold and clearing it out only took a total of five months. It felt to me like all of this had been orchestrated by the Divine. My mother's passing left me feeling blessed that I was able to be there and support her journey of transition right to the last moment.

CHAPTER SIXTEEN

SEDONA MAGIC

After my mother's house was sold and cleared out, I had my car packed to drive back to my community in Nevada City, California, where I once had my retreat center and wanted to visit my old community of friends.

Right before departing for Nevada City, California, from Salt Lake City, Utah, I received a call from my dear girlfriend, Colleen, who had lived in Nevada City when I did. I had not been in touch with my friends while I was in India living at the ashram. Shortly after I answered the phone, she invited me to stay in her home across from Thunder Mountain in Sedona, Arizona. I had not even known she and her husband had sold their beautiful Nevada City home and bought a home in Sedona as well as another one in Colorado on a river. I had my car packed to drive to California but when I "tuned in" to her invitation I was surprised when I received a great big "YES!" This is how I got to Sedona!

I had visited Sedona once when Ben was young, but it didn't grab me like it did this time. The majestic beauty and power of the mountains and their energy spoke to my soul. One of the first things I did upon arriving in Sedona was to attend an all-day drum-making workshop. A drum is a sacred tool that connects heaven and earth and relationships to all. It is the heartbeat of the spirit; leader of the people; and its vibrations connect throughout all time and space. Before beginning to make our drums, our group explored a powerful vortex site where we prayed and danced there. We became conscious of what we were letting go of and what we were calling into our lives. Upon returning to the retreat center, we chose our deer hides and were given wooden frames onto which we wrote our intentions. We infused our drums with our intentions and prayers while making them in silence. It was an amazing experience. I felt like I was setting the tone for living in Sedona. It was, in some sense, calling my life into being here.

While staying at my friend's home, I would hike to the top of lower Chimney Rock at both sunrise and sunset each day to do my Nama Japa with my Mala beads from India, silently chanting "Om Ma." I constantly live in a feeling of gratitude; thank you, beloved Sedona, for bringing me to this magical mystical place. I love living in Sedona. It resonates in my heart and soul. In Divine Feminine circles, the definition of the word sovereign I have often heard is: "whole unto herself." I now feel my sovereignty; an important part of this book is how I claimed it.

Once on a hike near my home in Sedona, I reflected back on a time in India when I had just arrived at Rishikesh. I was staying at the Ayurvedic Center; a friend from Nevada City had highly recommended an astrologer in Rishikesh. I heard from my friend that the actor Will Smith had gone to him for a reading. It was located only a 20-minute car ride away, but was a complicated appointment to make. I needed to give a deposit for the reading, which required me to go twice to his hard-to-find office. The whole reading was only $30! During the reading, he said I would be living in the Southwest United States, and I thought he was crazy for saying this. My plan at that time was to live in India for the rest of my life in service to Anandamayi Ma.

So here I am in Sedona, in the Southwest part of the United States. I've never experienced anything like this in my entire life. I feel as if the Divine has brought me here. In the evenings, the nearby beautiful red and white sandstone mountains just to the east of my home turn a deep red and purple with the hues of the setting sun. After, there's a golden glow intertwined with the purple before everything goes dark for the night. All I can do is sit on my deck and stare in awe. It is beyond deep beauty; it's as if the sun activates something in the mountains – they come absolutely alive. I come alive. I thank God-Goddess, with all my heart, that I am here. I love my home and where it is located, near the heart vortex chakra of Sedona. I can walk out my front door and in a few moments I'm on the trails. When it is warm, I walk barefoot to ground myself, and connect with the Earth. I have three favorite trees I love with all my heart.

One tree is absolutely beautiful, the way it is spread out. There is a limb that feels like it was made just for me, I can plop down on this limb that is narrow and yet it holds me like a hammock. When I walk, I collect heart rocks; Sedona is filled with them. I have placed many of the heart rocks all around my favorite trees and spots.

Another tree I like to hike to is far off the beaten path. It was the first tree I started to collect and leave heart rocks at. It is my very favorite mediation spot.

While hiking one afternoon, I met a young woman hugging a tree. Interested in what she was doing I asked her, and she replied, "This is The Hugging Tree; you can hug her and she will energetically hug you back!" After that initial meeting we would often run into each other on the trails. I now have The Hugging Tree's entire circumference surrounded with all sizes of heart rocks, some leaning on the tree, some lying on the ground, but every inch of the area is covered in heart rocks. Within a couple of feet, I have another plot of heart rocks lying on the ground. They are laid out randomly with the large and small heart rocks next to each other. On one of the larger heart rocks resting against the tree, there are sap droppings from the tree onto the stone. As the sunlight hits the drops, they look like pure golden jewels.

This is the particular tree where I chose to bury my mother's ashes. I did it on an equinox with a dear friend. We hiked to the top of Sugarloaf, the heart chakra of Sedona — and a vortex — with my drums, rattles, and all my sacred paraphernalia early in the morning, where I made prayers to the seven directions; East, West, North, South, sky, earth and within. I always feel it's a huge acknowledgment of some unseen forces that are grateful to us for taking this time out to honor the Earth, the solstices, and the equinoxes.

We hiked back down to the hugging tree, I dug a hole with a sharp rock, placed my mother's ashes inside, and covered the hole, saying prayers. I placed a very large heart rock over her resting spot. When

I concluded the ceremony, I had several bees hovering in front of my face reminding me of the time at Athena's Temple in Greece. I like to visit this tree and I like to visit my mother there. It makes me feel grateful that her ashes and this sacred tree are close together.

Winter is restful, but Spring is alive and full of life, and I love keeping my screen door open. The sun shines into my house, and it's actually warm. The world seems to wake up in Spring. Trees begin to fill with blossoms, the desert blooms with flowers, and birds such as robins, cardinals and bluejays are singing with all their hearts. I love the birdcall of the finches who have a nest in one of my trees. All year long we have ravens. Butterflies have reappeared. It feels like I could wake up just like Sleeping Beauty in this fully alive and powerful energy that becomes intensified by Spring here. All that was dormant during the Winter is now powerfully coming back to its full life-force with such exquisite beauty. Spring is filled with joy, new life, and new possibilities. It is a dynamic time. Perhaps because my birthday is in the early Spring, my life force also awakens from the stillness of Winter.

I was sitting outside on my deck daydreaming when my phone rang. It was Neha, my dear friend and dentist from India. She had always said she would never marry. But now she was saying, "Kathleen, I am getting married and you have to come to my wedding." I said, "Oh, but India is so far away." She said, "Kathleen, you have to come to my wedding, I want you here." I replied "Absolutely, I will be there." Her wedding would take place over five days. What an incredible experience! She lived 10 minutes from the ashram I had lived at. I emailed SwamiJi and Sarabjeeet, asking if I could stay at my home while I was there for her wedding. The reply: "It's your house; do what you want." With that cold response I realized I would not be staying at the ashram.

I was in India for a few weeks. Neha found a beautiful place for me to stay just a two-minute walk from her house. The retired doctor who owned the home refused to let me pay him! Each morning, I would walk to her house and spend the day helping and participating with the wedding activities. One day we had to go to Indore, the nearest large city, for shopping. I needed to purchase five outfits for the five days of the wedding ceremony. We left early in the morning and arrived back at midnight with the car full, and we did not complete all the shopping we needed to do! In fact, I had only found one outfit. We had more shopping to do later! Over the next few days, we spent many hours wrapping the presents she would be giving Raj, her husband-to-be.

All the women close to the bride got mendi, a henna paste, applied on their skin for her wedding ceremony. I had it applied to my hands and midway up my forearm, the design was so delicate and beautiful.

On one of the nights of the celebration there was a talent show. I had been told I would do a dance and three young women would teach it to me, but there wasn't enough time and I hadn't finished learning all the dance steps. That night I was to perform with these young women who were my instructors. I told Neha I was not going to do it because everyone was so talented, and I felt inadequate. She said, "follow your heart," and as I sat there watching the other performers, I remembered something a 5 Rhythms Dance teacher once said to me in a workshop: "Kathleen, getting up and doing this is an act of love, not a performance." This was an act of love to Neha and Raj, not a performance of being perfect! I had so much fun up on the stage with the other young women knowing this was truly an act of pure love.

We stayed overnight at a hotel for the wedding and reception in Omkareshwar. In the early evening Raj rode up on a white horse, dressed in all white with a white turban on his head, and fashionable black sunglasses. There were 40 drummers as part of the ceremony, and the loud beat of the drums was so primal, it is a moment I will remember for the rest of my life. The wedding was beautiful.

I had thought the ashram was my family, but my true family in India turned out to be Neha and her family. I visited the ashram and the atmosphere with Sarabjeet and SwamiJi was still extremely cold. I had brought three-pounds of chocolates for the boys and everyone at the ashram. I never had an opportunity to distribute it. I just left the candies there, leaving in tears. My experience at the ashram this time was a final acknowledgement of my unhappiness and choosing to relinquish it.

I returned to Sedona, and I was so happy to be back. Although things with the ashram did not work out, the wedding overshadowed all the pain and sorrow I felt from my visits to the ashram. Very shortly after my return I wrote a short email to SwamiJi and Sarabjeet, pointing out it was obvious to all of us this was no longer a fit. I asked them to please sell my home and return the $10,500 I had paid for it. It has now been over a year and I have never heard a word from them. We will see if they do this. It is in their hands and is their karma.

About a week later I had the final of my three sessions with the healing practitioner I had seen before going to India. Even though I have spent many years of my life working with some of the best healers in their respective fields, this was a monumental session for me. It seems like there are always layers upon layers, like those Russian nesting dolls. In this last session with her, time disappeared and suddenly we were enveloped by light with our light bodies communicating to each other. In all the years of healing adventures, I have never journeyed to such profound corners of my psyche. Once our session ended, she told me, "Kathleen, you claimed your sovereignty when you left your key inside your house at the ashram." She continued, "In all my years as a practitioner, you're the first I have witnessed claim their sovereignty, and the only person I have been able to say this to."

Living in Sedona now, I continue to go out and do amazing things with my friends. We love to get together and share experiences. It's profound to me how much support and love I get to participate in. Many events are based on music, creation, fully becoming, and celebrating with some of the most phenomenal people I have ever met. My heart is filled with immense joy living here.

I am equally blessed to know that my son Ben is deeply happy in his life. I raised Ben with love. He became a man of confidence and love, never needing to prove anything.

Ben lives overseas with his beautiful partner, Cecilia, who is a fashion designer, and they have a gorgeous boy, my grandson Sture, who at the time of my writing this is a toddler. I celebrate Ben and Cecilia's relationship. They share responsibility for raising their child in a relationship free from sexual, emotional, and mental abuse. Instead, they live from mutual respect, love, kindness, and support for each other. Theirs is a true and equal partnership. I see how he has broken the chains of my traumas.

Thank you, Ben, for being my teacher and breaking the chain of our ancestral traumas. You are my light on how to walk softly and carry internal power. You are truly being who you are. I admire you with all my heart and soul. Ben is a fantastic son, partner, and father!

Author's Reflections:

> "Healing does not mean that an issue will never hurt you again—Healing means that hurt will never control you again." — Unknown Author.

Through writing this book I have consciously seen and broken my vow of unhappiness. I now claim my happiness! I choose and deserve to be completely happy as does every person on our precious planet Earth.

Sharing and living my story has been an initiation; a Rite of Passage from being a victim of my unhealed traumas to a Sovereign woman. I am grateful for all the time I have spent healing. I can now look back on my dysfunctional family, marriage, and India experiences, as the catalysts of change. Like a kaleidoscope rearranging the fractals of my life. I have always been compelled to dive deeper into myself and the desire to make sense of my life was always paramount.

Just like the quote I shared at the beginning of my story, "The difficult I can do immediately; the impossible takes a little longer." This story reflected the journey of healing and becoming a sovereign woman.

I share this poem in support of your healing journey:

> Give yourself more credit. You're trying to grow while trying to Heal. You're trying to forgive while trying to grieve. You're trying to search while trying to let go. You're trying to love others while remembering how to love yourself. You're doing the best you can." Anonymous

Learning to live from the indomitable heart where love awakens to love can get you through the hardest of times. It can open up extraordinary experiences and opportunities, and break the chain of old ways of being in the world.

> *I now walk forward knowing*
> *I live in the Light of my power*
> *I accept who I am*
> *I trust life*

-*Kathleen Plant Lov*

With an overflowing heart I can say:

> My Indomitable Heart awakened to more Love and
> WE BROKE THE CHAIN!

APPENDIX

POWERFUL PRACTICES

SELF LOVE:

One of the most powerful practices I know is so simple but something we often don't do. It is SELF LOVE. What makes you feel loved... a hot bubble bath? Reading a favorite author? Eating an ice-cream cone? Doing something playful? Visiting your favorite art gallery? Talking on the phone to a dear friend? Look into your heart and make a list of Self Love things that you would love to do! And then start doing them. First thing in the morning I do a daily practice of touching each part of my body starting with my hair and saying "I love you, I thank you, I appreciate you;" going on to every part of my body and then imagining all the organs and glands and bones etc. on the inside. And ending with "Blessed am I to be a woman/man living in such a beautiful temple." That practice came from Dana Dharma Devi Delong.

What we feel inside gets radiated out. That FEELING is a magnet that attracts those same feelings back to you. This is very exciting because we choose what we want and then cultivate that feeling within us. It is then attracted back to us from the outside.

GRATITUDE JOURNAL:

I keep a journal just for gratitude. Every day I make a list of five things for which I am grateful. By keeping this journal, you start keeping your focus on gratitude!

WONDER:

Wonder is a powerful tool. I love to start out my day with, "I wonder how many people I am going to have the opportunity to really love and see today. I Wonder! I wonder how many amazing, incredible, magical, miraculous things are going to occur in my life before I go to bed tonight. I WONDER!!" What is it that you wonder?

TAKING YOURSELF ON A DATE:

Think of things you love to do. Once a week (or more often) you can take yourself on a date. You can go by yourself to a movie, an art gallery, explore someplace you have never been, do something fun and playful. What lights up your heart? Make a list and keep adding to it!

FORGIVING YOURSELF:

If you make a mistake, be gentle on yourself. Forgive yourself. Learning can often come by making mistakes before we get it right.

HO'OPONOPONO:

A Hawaiian practice of reconciliation and forgiveness
The words are:
"I'm sorry
Please forgive me
Thank you
I love you"

You can say it to someone you feel you have harmed in some way or for someone you feel harmed you in some way. It is so simple but very, very powerful. I repeat it over and over and over again.

LEARN SOMETHING NEW:

I had some friends visiting and they had an app where they could record the sound of a bird and it would tell them the name of that bird and interesting information about it. The other day I was sitting by a tree in my backyard where there were birds and a nest and the most unusual bird sounds I had ever heard. I purchased the app and found out they were finches!

I have also recently started taking a ceramics class. I started with the wheel but felt as a beginner there was too much to remember. I switched over to hand ceramics and found I loved the slowness and meditation working with the clay without the wheel. I feel so grateful to connect to Mother Earth in this way and have beautiful things that come from it!

BE KIND TO YOURSELF:

Be gentle and kind to yourself. Just like you would be with a child. Take care of your precious inner child too!

PLAYDATE WITH YOUR INNER CHILD:

What did you love to do as a child? I loved to play jacks for hours by myself and also loved pick-up-sticks. So, I keep these in my home to play with my inner child. Look at ways you can nurture and play with your precious inner child.

These are just a few suggestions from things that I personally do. I am sure there are books out there and many things you can find online to go even deeper. ENJOY!!

Blessings on your journey to your Self Love!

Love,
Kathleen Plant Lov

Gratitude to the people who helped me with my book.

Thank you to my dear friend Kerani Marie, who is an amazing artist, teacher, wise woman and author. She helps people write their books. She came to me at the very end as I was finishing my book. She was able to ask me deep questions that elicited more emotion in my book. It also brought my book alive in a deeper way. She helped connect the chapters with more fluidity.